*The Mississippi Experience*

# THE MISSISSIPPI EXPERIENCE

*Strategies for Welfare Rights Action*

**EDITED BY PAUL A. KURZMAN**
*With Foreword by George A. Wiley*

## CONTRIBUTORS

Ronald M. Arundell

Judith Beyman

Paul A. Kurzman

Barbara A. Schram

Ted Seaver

Heather Smith

Jeffrey R. Solomon

Gardenia White

ASSOCIATION PRESS • New York

THE MISSISSIPPI EXPERIENCE

Copyright © 1971 by the Michael Schwerner Memorial Fund, Inc.
Association Press, 291 Broadway, New York, N.Y. 10007

Articles previously published are acknowledged in a footnote on their first page. Articles not so credited were written especially for this volume.

### SPECIAL NOTE

The names of local Mississippians have been changed
to preserve anonymity.

Standard Book Number: 8096-1816-8

Library of Congress Catalog Card Number: 77-152896

PRINTED IN THE UNITED STATES OF AMERICA

 72

*Dedicated to the memory of*

**JAMES  CHANEY**

**ANDREW  GOODMAN**

**MICHAEL  SCHWERNER**

*and all those whose names we do not know*

# Contents

## *Part III.*  CASE STUDIES

## *Part IV.*  PRACTICE DILEMMAS

# *Foreword*

On a hot June day in 1965 I walked with a group of local residents of Philadelphia, Mississippi, down the long dusty road that led to the burned-out ruins of the church that James Chaney, Michael Schwerner, and Andrew Goodman visited on the day they were murdered. It was the first anniversary of the brutal slaying of these three civil rights workers—and a fitting memorial it was. A march led by the black leaders of Philadelphia, Mississippi, from the office set up shortly after the murders; a march involving the local people who had organized a Philadelphia branch of the Freedom Democratic Party and were carrying on the work that these young civil rights workers had begun.

It is similarly fitting that social workers in New York and across the nation have formed an ongoing memorial to Michael Schwerner—a young white social worker who had dedicated his life to organizing in a rural, hostile Mississippi. The Michael Schwerner Memorial Fund has supported an ongoing organizing base in Hinds County, Mississippi, and has maintained the spirit of the 1964 summer project by supporting social work summer interns in Mississippi who work with permanent organizers there. The Hinds County Welfare Rights Organization has been by far the most

9

important product of the Schwerner Fund's efforts over the past five years. Schwerner Fund organizers not only have acted as advocates for poor people in adjusting thousands of grievances against the Mississippi Welfare Department, but, through the Welfare Rights Organization, they have trained recipients in the techniques of welfare rights organizing and advocacy.

This book which chronicles the experiences of a number of Schwerner Fund workers in Mississippi is yet another contribution to the building of a truly living memorial to Michael Schwerner and the other civil rights heroes of the 60's. This book should become an important basic reference for social work students interested in community organization and for anyone seriously interested in the mechanics of community organizing. It will be especially helpful for whites working in an alien culture of blacks, Puerto Ricans, Chicanos, or on Indian reservations. This is so because of the extensive treatment of the problem of psychological preparation for work in a foreign environment. This of course may limit the utility of the volume to black or Spanish organizers working in their own communities. One should not, however, permit this to blind him to the wealth of valuable information and techniques that the papers contain.

For those who are new to community organization, the book probably reads best by starting with some of the case studies such as "The Porter Family Social Study" which describes Mrs. Edna Wilson Porter, mother of seven children, sharecropper, civil rights worker, on welfare with an income of $65 a month to support an entire family. Or, you can start with "The Case of Mrs. Susie T." in which a social work student begins to find out about life as it really is in Mississippi.

One could then proceed to the three papers in Part IV which set forth the diaries of three summer workers; two white and one black. From these, one begins to get the feel of the problems and early work that went into the organizing of the Hinds County Welfare Rights Organization.

One could then proceed to the papers by Ronald Arundell and Barbara Schram who ably set forth the basic framework for welfare rights organizing in Hinds County. Miss Schram adds useful material on ways in which whites can begin to get beyond self-awareness and discipline in her discussion of "The Conscious Use of Color: Some Attitudes and Roles for White Workers." Gardenia White does similar service around the issues of professionalism in her brief look at roles and relationships of paraprofessionals "down South and up South."

Finally, in Part I, Paul Kurzman and Jeffrey Solomon move from the nitty-gritty of the organizing experience to developing a theoretical framework. Dr. Kurzman goes further by creatively applying Fanon's analysis of relationships between colonized and colonizer/oppressed and oppressor.

Perhaps the most lively and interesting piece is Ted Seaver's "The Care and Feeding of Southern Welfare Departments" in which he combines perceptive analysis of southern welfare operations with deft and imaginative ideas of how to outwit the system.

*The Mississippi Experience* should serve as an excellent tool both for beginning organizers and students of community organization and for more experienced practitioners in the field. The material here will find valuable application not only in classrooms but in training courses for organizers in welfare rights and in other kinds of community organization as well. It is especially commended to anyone seeking a beginning knowledge of what welfare organizing is all about. But, since the welfare rights model might well be applied with certain modifications to tenant organizing, community unions, parent action, etc., the material should be valuable to organizers in other fields as well. For students, VISTA's, Peace Corpsmen, social workers, for blacks who wonder if whites are ever going to begin to understand the problems, for whites who are beginning to understand the problems, for Middle Americans who are trying to get out of the middle, *The Mississippi Experience* is well worth reading.

It is unfortunate that the book does not have any papers by the recipient leaders who have emerged from the Hinds County Organization. The volume would have been greatly enhanced by the inclusion of a piece by Norma Jean Williams, a leader of the Hinds County Welfare Rights Organization, or Geraldine Smith, who rose through the ranks of that organization to become Financial Secretary for the National Welfare Rights Movement. However, these might properly be the subject of a future volume.

This book catalogues important episodes in the building of a local welfare rights organization and documents a process repeated hundreds of times over in the development of the grass-roots base of the more than 700 welfare rights chapters which make up the National Welfare Rights Organization. It was by virtue of the painstaking nurture of these processes and linking up the local organizations on a nationwide basis that the first national organization of poor people since the 1930's was built. It will only be through the refinement and expanded use of these techniques that a broad-based "poor people's" movement of major political significance will be built in the United States.

DR. GEORGE A. WILEY

# Preface and Acknowledgments

In the summer of 1964 in Mississippi, three young men lost their lives in the fulfillment of their duties as civil rights workers in the Voter Registration Project. Their mission to assist fellow citizens to exercise the right to vote guaranteed by the Constitution ended abruptly, but the inspiration of their sacrifice to ensure the liberties of other men has endured.

In that same year, social workers identified with the cause of human rights created the Michael Schwerner Memorial Fund, Inc., a nonprofit, tax-exempt corporation, as a tribute to Michael Schwerner and to continue the work in which he, Andrew Goodman and James Chaney were engaged. The purpose of the Fund has been to provide social work services in Southern communities on behalf of civil rights.

For the past six years the Schwerner Fund has sponsored the Community Development Agency to serve the poor people of Hinds County, Mississippi. Their goal has been to provide some direct service, and to serve as organizers with and in the black community. In addition, for three summers the Fund sponsored Summer Social Work Training Institutes whereby northern social workers and social work students have volunteered to serve with the Community Development

Agency (CDA) for periods of from two weeks to two months. The costs for these institutes have been underwritten by foundations who have recognized the value of this experience—both to the people whom the CDA serves, and to the workers and students who have come to learn new skills and new forms of social work practice. This book is a product of the experiences of these workers and the CDA staff, present and past.

Let us remember that it all started with Mickey, who, with his co-martyrs—Goodman and Chaney—paid the ultimate price in order that we might begin to see our responsibilities. Their contributions should not be mentioned in the same breath with any others.

Those who have carried the burden of responsibility for the work of the Fund in Mississippi deserve special mention. Geraldine Smith, Jimmie Neal Haley, James Mays, Jesse Montgomery, Heather Smith and Ted Seaver have served on the front lines over the long months and years; they have given continuity and devotion to the work that had to be done. And the volunteers themselves who have served with them for the past few summers have provided the social work presence of which we so often speak and yet seldom acknowledge.

The New York Foundation and the Aaron E. Norman Fund have stepped in to provide the financial support that has made possible the experiments we have undertaken. To these foundations who have supported us in this new venture goes a sense of deep respect and appreciation.

A special word of recognition also is due those social workers who have served generously as chairmen of the Schwerner Fund's Board of Directors. To Dr. Rita A. McGuire and Dr. Hyman J. Weiner, past co-chairmen, and to Mrs. Susan K. Kinoy and Preston R. Wilcox, present co-chairmen, goes a profound sense of gratitude for the committed leadership they have provided. It was Preston Wilcox, moreover, who organized the first summer volunteer experience, and lent his inspiration to the volunteers who went south. Finally, to the members of the Board of Directors and Mississippi Project Committee who lent their time, both down South and up South as well, we acknowledge their quiet contribution to the success of the work we have undertaken.

P. A. K.

New York City

# *Introduction*

All of the material in this book is derived from field experience of the Michael Schwerner Memorial Fund's Community Development Agency in Jackson, Mississippi. The primary goal here is to funnel their practice experience back into social work education and training.

Most of the articles have been written by social workers and social work students who served as summer volunteers with the Community Development Agency during the summers of 1967 through 1969. Each volunteer was part of a Summer Training Institute, developed by the Schwerner Fund with the following goals:

1) To provide services to the black poor. There is almost a total absence of social service for black people—from public transportation, to medical attention; from adequate assistance from the departments of public welfare, to service from the nationally supported private welfare institutions.

2) To work toward strengthening blacks in this setting so that they may carry on the fight for their share of income and institutional services long after the volunteers have gone —so that the children of these families will not have to turn up as clients of these same volunteers years later in the North.

3) To help social work students, graduate social workers

and paraprofessionals understand the rural backgrounds and life-styles of the black poor in the Deep South.

4) To expose young workers and students to the racism of which the Kerner Commission has spoken—and which can be seen so easily in the polarization of rich and poor, oppressor and oppressed, that characterizes Hinds County, Mississippi. If racism is the basic sickness of America, this is indeed the clinic in which it may be seen, raw and blatant. These insights can be transferred to the northern setting.

5) To collect data (including record material) which may prove decisive in documenting local conditions and formulating public policy; in providing new teaching material for schools of social work; and in contributing to the dialogue about the role of social workers as advocates for social change.

One of the unusual aspects of this volume is the variety in both content and style—a professional eclecticism, if you will —which the editor has made every effort to preserve. But each article does tend to focus on broad social issues and fundamental policy questions which are at the heart of the social work experience.

Part I presents articles that attempt to frame a theoretical approach that threads throughout the volume. Part II gives examples of some creative social work techniques and new models for practice. Part III offers case studies of particular interest to methods courses. Part IV provides a series of insights from the daily experiences of workers facing unusual practice dilemmas.

At the conclusion of each article, "Study Questions" are posed which may prove helpful in a teaching or training situation. These questions seek to make the reader look more closely at the ideas and issues implicit in the paper, as well as at the worker's practice. Hence, with a traditional stress on the development of practice skills goes an equally strong emphasis on developing the reader's acumen in the social policy arena.

*The Mississippi Experience* therefore is more than a book of readings; hopefully it is a vehicle for learning, teaching and training. It is designed to make the reader puzzle and doubt, accept and reject, question and wonder—for this is how he acquires fresh skills and absorbs new knowledge. The authors are committed toward these goals; and they will be grateful if they have been in part successful.

*PART I*

# THE
# CONCEPTUAL
# FRAMEWORK

# The Native-Settler Concept: Implications for Community Organization

PAUL A. KURZMAN

Those community organization practitioners who have worked with low-income blacks in the Deep South or with recent southern immigrants to the large urban ghettos of the North have begun to recognize an organizational problem and to search for a solution. The problem, especially acute in the South, is that the brand of militant confrontation that has been so successful for whites and northern blacks does not seem to be as comfortable a pattern of response for blacks today in the South. It was not by chance that Martin Luther King chose the technique of passive resistance, just as Gandhi deliberately used it in India's confrontation with the British. Yet with all of the apparent gains that King wrought in Birmingham and Atlanta, for example, one does not have to be in these cities long to see that in everyday life the essential plight of the southern black has not been improved substantially. While, for example, there is nominal integration of the police and fire departments in a city as relatively liberal

Adapted with permission of the National Association of Social Workers from *Social Work,* Vol. 14, No. 3 (July, 1969), pp. 58–64.

as Atlanta, this is mere tokenism and does not represent equality throughout these departments even by northern standards.

The statistics are there to be read. By June 1968 only 14 per cent of black students in the eleven Deep South states were attending integrated classes. This means that fourteen years after the 1954 Supreme Court decision, approximately 86 per cent of black pupils in the South were still in segregated schools.[1] Although they represent almost 12 per cent of the national population, blacks have been unable to elect even one person to the hundred-member U.S. Senate. (Senator Edward Brooke of Massachusetts was elected from a state with a 97.5 per cent white population, and he made it clear that he would not be representing the black cause.) Since Reconstruction not one member of the national legislature from the eleven Deep South states has been Negro. In 1967 the legislative body stripped Adam Clayton Powell (the only black legislator ever to achieve a committee chairmanship) of a post it had taken his ghettoed constituents twenty years to acquire. A bitter black community watched as a white congressman, guilty of far more serious charges, was reluctantly chided after an "investigation" in which much damaging evidence was withheld.[2] Well-meaning Americans habitually apply an irrational double standard when they ponder black people or racial problems. Says black psychiatrist Alvin F. Poussaint:

This is not surprising, since Americans come from a heritage in which signers of the Declaration of Independence that avowed "all men are created equal" were in fact slave owners, and few white citizens saw the contradiction.[3]

[1] Marjorie Hunter, "A Lag in Schools of South Decried," *New York Times*, October 16, 1968, p. 19. These figures were compiled by the U.S. Department of Health, Education and Welfare.

[2] Ernest Dunbar, "Memo from the Ghetto: The Dispirit of '67," *Look*, September 19, 1967, p. 92.

[3] "The White Press Distorts Race News," *New York Times*, November 12, 1967, Sect. IV.

## Native-Settler Relationship

What has happened, then, is that conditions today in the segregated urban ghettos and in most of the Deep South resemble *apartheid*. As in the Union of South Africa, the relationships between blacks and whites are carefully governed, if not by law, by long-standing sets of informally maintained traditions. In the absence of strong federal laws and firm enforcement, the weight of tradition is frequently as strong as the weight of the law.

There are basically two types of people, the ins and the outs—or, in the words of Negro psychoanalyst Frantz Fanon, the "settler" and the "native."[4] Fanon, in a study of the revolution in North Africa that won independence for Algeria a few years ago, emphasizes the native-settler relationship as a key to understanding the perpetuation of colonialism in Algerian society.[5] He goes on to indicate why he feels it was the native's ability to break the bonds of this relationship that permitted him to revolt successfully and establish self-government and independence.

If we are willing for a moment to admit that there are some parallels between the condition of black people in the Deep South today and the slave-master relationship of colonial Africa (and indeed of America before the Emancipation), we may find Fanon's ideas relevant to an understanding of the difficulty southern blacks experience in trying to break free. In light of the conditions in the South today that have just been outlined and the black people's long history of slavery and quasi-servitude prior to the civil rights movement of this decade, there would seem to be reason to explore the

[4] Fanon uses the terms "settler" and "native" to connote the oppressor and the oppressed. Rather than adhering to a historical definition, Fanon is concerned (as the writer is) with the psychological dynamics that seem to govern the relationship between "settlers" and "natives"—i.e., master and servant, oppressor and oppressed.

[5] Frantz Fanon, *The Wretched of the Earth* (New York: Grove Press, 1966).

parallel further. Even in 1971, for the majority of whites and blacks in the South a double standard exists, and the native-settler relationship continues to dominate the informal structure known as the "southern way of life."

In fact, Fanon says that there are certain bonds that tie the ins and the outs, the settler and the native: First is a symbiotic need for each other. While it is easy to see why the native is dependent on the settler, it must not be forgotten that dependency works both ways.[6] A second relationship is charity: the settler's desire to keep the natives "off the streets," to make them the "invisible poor."[7] The third and most important link between the two is that of force—of violence, if you will. As Gunnar Myrdal perceptively notes, the principal point of contact between the two is the police, who through violence or—equally effective—the threat of violence maintain the status quo and keep the relationship stable and intact.[8]

## *The* Negeya *Bond*

From years of living this way the native learns to adapt in order to minimize punishment and maximize pleasure. He comes to see himself as he is seen by others.[9] He is bound by

[6] Douglas Turner Ward's powerful play, *A Day of Absence,* told of the dependence of the settler on the native in a way few had the courage to recognize before. Ward portrayed the helplessness of southern whites on a day when all local blacks left town, including a poignant satire of a white woman who suddenly realized she did not know how to cook or to care for her children, because she had never before had to do these things. *See* William Couch, Jr., ed., *New Black Playwrights* (Baton Rouge: Louisiana State University Press, 1968), pp. 25–60.

[7] Michael Harrington, *The Other America* (New York: Macmillan Co., 1962).

[8] *An American Dilemma: The Negro Problem and Modern Democracy* (New York: Harper & Row, 1962), p. 535.

[9] *See* "the self-fulfilling prophecy" in Robert K. Merton, *Social Theory and Social Structure* (Glencoe, Ill.: Free Press, 1957); and a more specific application in Thomas F. Pettigrew, *A Profile of the Negro American* (Princeton, N.J.: D. Van Nostrand Co., 1964).

what the Vietnamese term the "*Negeya* (neg-ee'-ya) bond."
Briefly, this means that in order to explain his own condition,
the native sees the settler as "having the will of God." The
will of God is preordained and therefore is not to be dis-
turbed. In a primitive society that is tradition bound, such
conclusions are common.

Even a brief visitor to the Deep South will be struck by
the parallel. Today, as in the past, tradition plays a strong
part in the black man's (the native's) way of life. Superstitions are rampant and religion plays a dominant role in
explaining phenomena from poor health to poor roads. Every
meeting, no matter how small, opens with a long series of
emotional prayers. If the settler (the white) has given the
native something extra for his bale of cotton, that he chose to
do so is attributed to "the will of God."

Traditional patterns are strong. All whites, even civil rights
workers who have worked side by side with blacks for more
than a year, are "Mr. Ted" or "Miss Barbara." If the white
worker makes a suggestion, it is right; for most blacks no
further effort to explore the idea more deeply seems necessary. In politics, while black candidates are being elected in
northern cities (where the "traditional" orientation and
*Negeya* bond do not prevail), Negro candidates in most
southern counties—even with black voting majorities—are
defeated. For example, in November 1967, a well-qualified
black candidate, Lofton Mason, ran for the office of beat
supervisor in Beat 2 of Jackson, Mississippi—an area in which
blacks represented 80 per cent of the population and 70
per cent of the registered voters—and lost.[10] (Long before
the election an experienced local observer predicted privately

[10] In Mississippi, counties are run essentially by a series of supervisors,
each elected from a "beat," or district, of which they will be in charge.
They have a great deal of power: they set the county taxes, hear appeals
from the county tax assessor, decide on the boundaries of the voting dis-
tricts in county elections, hire the county police, and control expenditure
of public moneys for everything from building roads to welfare. *See A
Political Handbook for the Black People of Jackson County* (Tougaloo,
Miss.: Freedom Information Service, 1967), p. 5.

to the author that Mason would lose.[11]) The opposing white candidate, although poorly qualified, had "the will of God." As one lifelong Negro resident of Beat 2 said, "Running a beat—that's white man's work."

Yet on that same Election Day, blacks Richard Hatcher and Carl Stokes won the mayoralties of Gary, Indiana, and Cleveland, Ohio. In Gary, black precincts supported Hatcher with 76 per cent of their votes; in Cleveland, Stokes received an estimated 94.5 per cent of the black votes cast.[12] In the nominally integrated northern city, where the native-settler relationship no longer prevails, the *Negeya* bond has long since been broken, and somehow the white candidates no longer have the will of God.

## Breaking the Bond

The important question for community organization is how the bond between native and settler in the Deep South can be broken. How can southern blacks achieve the personal freedom from traditional bonds and superstitions that can make democracy work for them today in the South? As a starting point, let us look to Frantz Fanon, and see what his thinking has been.

At the risk of oversimplification, Fanon feels that the crippling relationship of native and settler can only be destroyed by violence, because this has been the principal point of contact between the two. Fanon feels that the catharsis of absolute violence by the natives against their colonial oppressors will liberate the former from the bond of the *Negeya*.

The native cures himself of colonial neurosis by thrusting out the settler through force of arms. . . . When a peasant takes a gun in

[11] Ted Seaver, former coordinator of the Schwerner Fund operation in Mississippi, made this observation, which proved on Election Day to be perfectly correct. The author is indebted to Mr. Seaver for his many valuable observations on this paper and for his analysis of the significance of Fanon's concept and its nonviolent application through the symbolic act.

[12] Anthony Ripley and Donald Janson, "Stokes Picks White Aides: Hatcher Victory Certified," *New York Times*, November 9, 1967, p. 33.

his hands, the old myths grow dim and the prohibitions are one by one forgotten. . . . To shoot down a European is to kill two birds with one stone, to destroy an oppressor and the man he oppresses at the same time: there remains a dead man, and a free man; the survivor, for the first time, feels a national soil under his foot.[13]

Fanon tells the story of the native rebel preparing to overthrow his oppressive master, against cautions from his mother, who is bound by centuries of tradition. In a verse from the French poet Aimé Cèsaire, the rebel approaches the house where the master is smoking a pipe in the library surrounded by his trappings. The rebel is mesmerized by tradition for moments, then enters and, to the settler's surprise, plunges the knife decisively:

It was I, even I, and I told him so, the good slave, the faithful slave, the slave of slaves, . . . and I struck, and the blood spurted; that is the only baptism that I can remember today.[14]

"That's when I was born," he cries, "that's when I became a man."[15]

## Nonviolent Confrontation

Fanon, Styron, and the poet Cèsaire all comment on the same general phenomenon, which in psychiatric terms might

---

[13] The quotation above is by Jean-Paul Sartre, commenting on Fanon's ideas in the "Preface" to *The Wretched of the Earth, op. cit.,* pp. 18–19. Fanon himself says incisively, "The colonized man finds his freedom *in and through violence." Ibid.,* p. 67. (Italics mine.)

[14] Aimé Cèsaire, "Les Armes Miraculeuses," in Fanon, *op. cit.,* pp. 67–69.

[15] Fanon is not the only writer to tell of this "plunge-the-knife" phenomenon. William C. Styron, in his controversial *Confessions of Nat Turner* (New York: Random House, 1967), refers to the reaction of the formerly docile servant Hark after slaying his master: "A servant of servants was Hark no more; he had tasted blood."

While Styron's fictional account varies liberally from the text of Turner's *Confessions,* even Styron's critics do not appear to question the cathartic quality of these violent confrontations. *See* John H. Clarke, ed., *William Styron's Nat Turner: Ten Black Writers Respond* (Boston: Beacon Press, 1968).

be referred to as identification with the oppressor or turning against the self.[16] The natives have indeed been brainwashed or programmed into a way of life that assures their subservience to the settler, whom they see as somehow possessing the will of God. The relationship that traditionally binds native and settler to one another perpetuates the subservience of the native until, through a supreme act of confrontation and violence, he breaks this *Negeya* bond and emerges a man.

In so doing, the native is released from his traditional position or is, in effect, liberated and "deprogrammed." Blacks then no longer tone down their own aspirations or accept the inferiority attributed to them by the settler.

As Preston R. Wilcox has observed, Martin Luther King moved the natives toward freedom bestowed by the settler, but Malcolm X moved them toward liberation from a reliance on white sanctions. One can be technically "free" but not liberated; a liberated man is de facto free. Liberation is self-defined, self-bestowed, and self-earned.[17] Malcolm X, Stokely Carmichael, and Ron Karenga are all "deprogrammers" who stress the need for the natives to confront the settlers and to win their freedom—in all probability through an act of violence.[18]

The first requisite for the community organization worker among natives and settlers, then, is to recognize the existence

[16] *See* Charles Brenner, *An Elementary Textbook of Psychoanalysis* (Garden City, N.Y.: Doubleday & Co., 1955), p. 103; and Sigmund Freud, *Civilization and Its Discontents* (Garden City, N.Y.: Doubleday & Co., 1958), Chap. VII. *See also* the application of this psychiatric concept to the Negro question in Robert W. Friedrichs, "Interpretation of Black Aggression," *Yale Review*, Vol. 57, No. 3 (Spring, 1968), pp. 358–74.

[17] "So You Want To Be Black," *Black Caucus*, journal of the Association of Black Social Workers, Vol. 1, No. 1 (Fall, 1968), p. 34; or, *see Etcetera* Magazine, Vol. 1, No. 3 (July, 1969), p. 49. The author is grateful to Mr. Wilcox for his thoughtful and perceptive suggestions on this paper.

[18] *See* Malcolm X and Alex Haley, *The Autobiography of Malcolm X* (New York: Grove Press, 1966); Stokely Carmichael and C. V. Hamilton, *Black Power* (New York: Random House, 1967); and Ron Karenga, *The Quotable Karenga* (Los Angeles: US Organization, 1967).

of the *Negeya* bond and to see how it might be broken. The most pressing question is whether these bonds can truly be severed without the violence Fanon describes—and some contemporary civil rights organizers recommend.

Since we are not willing to advocate riots and violence, yet recognize the seriousness of the *Negeya* phenomenon, it is suggested that an attempt be made to re-create the native-settler encounter through nonviolent acts of confrontation. There appear to be three possible stages of confrontation: 1) At the earliest level, the role of professional community organization practitioner would be as actor-teacher, actually carrying out the symbolic confrontation in the presence of the native and on his behalf. 2) At the second level, the native himself would enact the confrontation, with the presence and active support of the worker, functioning as catalyst-team member. 3) Finally, the participating native, having begun to achieve a psychological breakthrough, would confront the settler directly, with the community organization worker in the background role of advocate-observer.[19] Although there would have to be a gradual process involved in progression from the first to the third stage, the writer believes that *the* Negeya *bond would not effectively be broken until the final stage had been reached and the act had been repeated by various natives with different settlers in a variety of settings.*

The confrontations, furthermore, must be personal, subjectively meaningful, symbolic acts of defiance. They must take place in a small group, and the native must get a sense of individual involvement. The leader must feel that he, with his fellow natives, is symbolically "plunging the knife."

[19] In moving through the three stages of confrontation, the ultimate goal would be to free the client of any need for or dependence on the worker. It should be understood, however, that this process probably would be gradual and require an ongoing social work assessment. In this regard, the new roles of actor-teacher, catalyst-team member, and advocate-observer may prove quite demanding on both the professional and adaptational skills of the worker.

Further, for positive reinforcement, the confrontation must be perceived as successful and catch the settler on his own grounds.

## The Mississippi Experience

Staff and volunteers with the Michael Schwerner Memorial Fund experimented with this on all levels in the summer of 1967 with some noteworthy results. On the earliest level, a professional organizer from the Schwerner Fund confronted an untrained racist welfare worker at a local social agency *in the presence and on behalf of a client*. The worker was so upset that she visibly shook, spoke openly like a racist, and was shattered when made to look foolish and incompetent by the organizer. The client looked on with silent satisfaction as the knife was effectively plunged and the worker squirmed in helpless exposure. Later the client could speak of nothing else for hours, and said, "I can take care of her next time— she's nothing but a nasty old woman."

Other examples of Stage 1 activity include the project coordinator's confrontations with welfare department supervisors at fair hearings. In the presence of the client and on her behalf, Schwerner Fund staff have made local welfare workers appear as foolish, inept, and arbitrary as so many of them are. Despite the quasi-judicial setting, the staff worker in almost every hearing has been able to create a cathartic confrontation, leaving the punitive hearing officers feeling helpless and breaking down the effectiveness of the *Negeya* bond. Some clients later took the staff worker's role in fair hearings on behalf of their fellow clients, thereby moving on to a Stage 2 confrontation.

In Stage 2 the natives act, but in the presence of and with the support of the organizer. One example in the 1967 summer experience was the integration of the bathrooms in a rural county courthouse. The clients, all black, resented having to use segregated toilets; they wanted to use the staff facilities, which were for whites only. With some trepidation, *but in the presence of and with the support of the organizer,* they went one by one to the staff bathroom, sustaining stares of disbelief from the whites present.

Examples of Stage 3 activities are much rarer in the Deep South, for this is why the *Negeya* bond has not yet been broken. There are a few new leaders emerging who have experienced or are ready to experience such symbolic confrontations. Most are young and frequently veterans of the civil rights activity of 1963–64; a few are products of the training and community development process that has been encouraged by such groups in Mississippi as the Freedom Democratic Party, Child Development Group of Mississippi, Michael Schwerner Memorial Fund, and the Delta Ministry.

## Significance for Theory and Practice

The process of placing the theory into a conceptual framework, which must effectively precede its systematic practice, has only begun. The experiences of Fanon in the Algerian revolution of the 1950's, of the slave rebellions in the South in the 1800's, and of black militants in the civil rights struggle in the 1960's now must be woven together and distilled for their significance to community organization theory and practice.

Several values would appear to accrue from achieving an understanding of the concept of the native and settler, apart from a much-needed refinement of its broader applicability.

1. It may provide an increased understanding of riots and other forms of ghetto violence. It is not hard to understand why Black Power advocates encourage the use of the "knife-plunging" technique on a mass scale: they are not only eager to gain attention for their demands; they also recognize the cathartic value of the experience of confrontation. In the long run, the value of the catharsis outweighs the wrath of the press, public officials, or the Congress—who represent settlers in the over-all scheme.

2. It is equally easy to explain why riots and similar acts of

violence are more common in northern ghettos than in the
Deep South. Where the *Negeya* bond is strongest, the native-
settler relationship will be most firmly established, and the
tradition of *apartheid* and segregation in the Deep South
effectively perpetuates the myth that the white man has the
will of God.

3. Most workers among low-income Negroes who are first-
generation migrants from the South will find the *Negeya*
bond still present, albeit in a subtler form. The bond is not
easily broken, even by moving North, except through confrontation. Most practitioners in the black ghetto can cite
numerous examples of their struggle with this elusive
phenomenon; the subtlety of its appearance in a more liberal
northern setting can make it in many ways more difficult to
handle there.

4. Most important of all is the possibility of using the
cathartic confrontation on all three stages *as a deliberate
community organization strategy.* As a first step, it would be
well to recognize that in all-black areas, especially those
closest to southern patterns of segregation and bondage, there
are special and discrete phenomena to which the trained
worker must be sensitized. There are special community
organization tools to be added to his generic equipment.

One could argue that the use of *black* organizers would
reduce two possible dangers: a) fostering dysfunctional
dependency of blacks on white workers; and b) permitting
growth of a destructive form of white paternalism. Although
it has not been proved as yet, one can say that it is entirely
possible, therefore, that exclusive use of black organizers
would speed the progress from Stage 1 to Stage 3 involvement. One can say, however, that the situation provides a
special challenge for any worker, who must have the willingness and ability to work within the limits of the native-settler
model.

It is possible that further practice refinement of the concept
may add to the growing literature of community organization

theory. Hoffman's theory of the "single-purpose leader," Minnis' power structure research, Whitaker's "divide-and conquer" concept, Wilcox's "deprogramming tool" and theory of "functional anger," and Seaver's "professional Mau Mau" are recent steps in the direction of building a new community organization theory out of practice experience.[20] It is hoped that the native-settler concept will provide still another contribution to the charting of social work theory.

STUDY QUESTIONS

1. Is it true that "the essential plight of the southern black man has not improved substantially"? Why? How about the plight of black people in the North?

2. What does Dr. Poussaint mean by the "irrational double standard" of well-meaning Americans?

3. Is the comparison of the situation (in our urban ghettos and in the Deep South) to *apartheid* really a valid one? Can the "weight of tradition" really be as strong as the "weight of law"?

4. Is there a "symbiotic need for each other" in the relationship between blacks and whites in the Deep South? Does the dependency work both ways? Explain.

5. In reference to Gunnar Myrdal's comment, how can violence be a source of social stability?

6. What is the meaning of Merton's "self-fulfilling prophecy"? Can you give other examples of this phenomenon from your practice experience?

[20] See Nicholas von Hoffman, *Finding and Making Leaders* (Nashville: Southern Student Organizing Committee, 1968); Jack Minnis, "The Care and Feeding of Power Structures," *New University Thought*, Vol. 4, No. 1 (Summer, 1964), pp. 73–79; William Whitaker, *In the Lion's Den* (Columbus, Ohio: Welfare Rights Organization, 1967); Wilcox, *op. cit.*, pp. 32–36; Wilcox, "Is Integration Relevant?" *Renewal* (August, 1966), pp. 3–4; Ted Seaver, "The Care and Feeding of Southern Welfare Departments," *infra*, Chapter 3.

7. Is the example of black candidates being elected in the North, and being defeated in the South, still valid? How about the election of Charles Evers in Fayette, Miss.?

8. Do you agree with Fanon that the crippling relationship between oppressor and oppressed can only be destroyed by violence? Defend your position.

9. What is the rebel really saying when he declares that the act of killing the settler is "the only baptism that I can remember today"? Psychologically, what happened to the rebel that gave him this feeling?

10. Define "identification with the oppressor" and "turning against the self"? Can you give examples from your previous reading or present practice?

11. What does Wilcox mean when he says that Martin Luther King "moved the natives toward freedom bestowed by the settler"? Do you agree with Wilcox that one "can be technically 'free' but not liberated"? Explain.

12. Do you believe that *re-creation* of the native-settler encounter through nonviolent acts of confrontation will be effective? Why?

13. Why does the author insist that the *Negeya* bond would not be broken until the third stage of confrontation has been mastered?

14. Why would the new roles of actor-teacher, catalyst-team member and advocate-observer be particularly demanding on the professional and adaptational skills of the worker?

15. Do you feel that the confrontation of the worker at the private social agency was appropriate? Helpful? Professional?

16. Explain why the coordinator's activities at fair hearings are able to create a "cathartic confrontation."

17. What are the similarities (and differences) between the slave rebellions of the 1800's, the Algerian revolution of the 1950's, and the civil rights struggle of the 1960's?

18. Why can the cathartic value of riots outweigh the wrath of the "system"? What is the psychological significance of a cathartic experience?

19. Do you agree that the relative subtlety of the *Negeya*

bond in the North makes it more difficult to handle? Explain your answer.

20. How do you feel about the merits of using white organizers in the black community? Do you think the exclusive use of black workers might speed the progress from Stage 1 to Stage 3 involvement?

21. Is the use of cathartic confrontation as a deliberate community organization strategy consistent with the goals and ethics of social work practice?

# Beyond Advocacy: Toward a New Model for Community Organization

JEFFREY R. SOLOMON

The role of community organization in social work is undergoing questioning and revision. The profession, seeking legitimization, insists that all its methods maintain a scientific form designed to conquer the variables which are omnipresent in human relationships. Community organization practitioners, who were rather recently accepted in the professional ranks, therefore attempt to devise techniques to make community organization a legitimate social work function. Consequently, community organization, like other social work methods, becomes more concerned with professional techniques and jargon than with the basic questions concerning effective practice.

Here we will attempt to deal with the dilemma of trying to maintain professionalism and still be creative and productive at the same time. We seek no one methodological approach to the problems of the community. Rather, we

Adapted with permission of the Columbia University Press from *Social Work Practice: 1970* (New York: Columbia University Press, 1970), pp. 65–73.

offer a means by which communities may be organized, seeking to utilize the most positive aspects of traditional social
work as well as newer approaches to community organization
method and practice. Implicit in this goal is the recognition
that, similar to social movements in contemporary America,
the professions too are gliding through a phase of "doing your
own thing," leaving in question the absoluteness of any community organization dogma. Social work, therefore, may now
be ready to test out doctrine in day-to-day practice and need.
This approach, analogous to *consensus fidelum* in the Church,
permits codification of the practice by the institution after
the fact. For example, Vatican II engaged in various forms of
*consensus fidelum* in regard to its positions, questioning much
of the past history. This was done in recognition of change
within religious institutions and secular society.

## The Advocacy Dilemma

Recent thinking within social work, including community
organization, provides what seems to be an irreconcilable
theoretical framework. On the one hand, the traditional social
worker espouses client self-determination growing to increasing client independence. On the other hand, one school of
thought in community organization calls for advocacy practice by the professional community organizer.[1] Charles
Grosser, for example, makes the analogy between the social
work advocate and the legal advocate, pointing out the professional ramifications of each. One essential difference
(requiring careful consideration if one is to utilize the advocate's role in social work) is the constraints of the social
agency. The profession of law traditionally is practiced on
the basis of the independence of each attorney in acting on
behalf of his clients. The exercise of any type of restraint on
an attorney's advocacy results in unconscionable, and perhaps unethical, practice. This is not necessarily the case in

[1] Charles Grosser, "Community Development Programs Serving the Urban Poor," *Social Work*, Vol. 10, No. 3 (July, 1965), pp. 15–21.

social work. Executives of agencies must be prepared for backlash when their staffs engage in advocacy. This backlash may come from professional colleagues, the community, the board of directors, or from sources of funding. How does the executive act when these pressures are upon him? Are there not additional constraints placed on an advocate by agency policies? Is this not a perversion of the legal principle of advocacy independence?

Mayer Zald points out the various factors that come into play in the daily operation of the community organization agency. He sees the practitioner not as a free agent, but rather as limited by the goals and politics of the agency.[2] This premise may be further expanded to include the agency executive, who sees himself as limited by the goals and politics of the agency board. In this connection, George Brager points out:

Social welfare organizations are socially dependent. Since they are not financially self-supporting, they must accommodate to relevant publics. A relationship inevitably exists between an organization's fund raising base and its willingness to press for institutional change. The class location and value commitments of the major donors are, of course, primary in this regard. Organizational decision making is thus affected by powerful community forces to which institutional change may be unsettling.[3]

Brager's contentions are relevant to the constraints placed upon the advocate model—constraints which generally are not permitted to be placed upon the law advocate (the basis of the social work model). Whether funding stems from the private or the public sector, prohibitions are placed on an agency which filter down to the practitioner.

While it might be ideal to have community organizers work in private practice like attorneys, in order to avoid

[2] Mayer Zald, "Organizations as Politics: An Analysis of Community Organization Agencies," *Social Work*, Vol. 11, No. 4 (October, 1966), pp. 56–65.

[3] George Brager, "Institutional Change: Perimeters of the Possible," *Social Work*, Vol. 12, No. 1 (January, 1967), p. 61.

some of these constraints, the economics of the practitioner-client relationship do not make such an alternative feasible at this point. A means of moving toward this direction, however, would be the institution of "Sociocare," which would entitle social work practitioners to the same remuneration received by physicians under Medicare.[4] In such a system, the social worker would be bound by client selection and the ethics of the profession rather than by the requirements of a social agency. It is a possible professional alternative to agency practice. Now is the time perhaps for the social work profession to recognize the advantages of private practice in community organization.

## The Dependency Dilemma

It seems to this writer that where true advocacy exists, client self-determination is difficult to implement, because the advocate generally determines the best course of action to achieve the client's end. Advocate determination rather than client determination tends to establish a client dependency upon the practitioner—which is counter to the tradition and goals of social work.

Further, it seems wasteful to establish a core of professionally trained advocates, when legal training is geared to provide the most effective confrontation expert. While the social work advocate has become a quasi-legal spokesman for the poor, he is functioning as such with only a few of the tools needed to meet his ends and the goals of the client. He is not a member of the bar, does not have the professional recognition accorded to an attorney, is unable to advocate in judicial settings, and has never received the exposure to legal procedures and rhetoric that is an integral part of a lawyer's training. It is essential, therefore, that we find the means of altering the traditional advocate role to bring advocacy closer to the ethic of social work.

[4] For further discussion, see Irving Piliavin, "Restructuring the Provision of Social Services," *Social Work*, Vol. 13, No. 1 (January, 1968), pp. 34–41.

## A Proposed Model

In the proposed model, three distinct worker roles are envisioned. They follow the historical development of a group, and the worker's transition from one role to the next is a key factor in his effectiveness as a practitioner and in his success in building a self-reliant community organization.

It might be noted that while it is advantageous to have the same worker play all three roles below (moving appropriately from one role to the next), the Mississippi experience of the Michael Schwerner Memorial Fund has indicated that different workers may practice at each of these junctures. The roles outlined below are those of organizer-advocate, organizer-educator, and organizer-technical assistant.

### Phase I: Worker as Organizer-Advocate.

The initial phase of the method entails utilization of the traditional advocate role as defined, for example, by Grosser. Here, the organizer takes on the function of an activist attorney, marshaling resources and arguing the case with, and on behalf of, his clients.

This role assumes that: 1) the worker can better achieve early victories than the client group; 2) the worker will maintain a lawyer-client relationship, i.e., compromising only when it is in the interest of the client; and 3) fears of the target system will begin to diminish as clients survive confrontation with the system, and—with their advocate's planful assistance—begin to win both real and symbolic victories.

This last point is extremely significant in organizing poor people, especially blacks in the Deep South. Paul Kurzman speaks of a *"Negeya* bond" which may exist between blacks and whites, natives and settlers, clients pushing for change and representatives of the target system.[5] The client feels that it is the will of God that makes the system control so

[5] Paul A. Kurzman, Chapter 1, *supra:* "The Native-Settler Concept: Implications for Community Organization."

much of his life, and therefore his acceptance of the existing order must systematically be broken down. The nature of involvement during Phase I permits the organizer-advocate to prove that change is indeed possible, and that no tragic outcome will stem from confrontation of the system. The client who has been brought up bound by this *Negeya* bond may begin to question its validity unless he sees that he and the advocate are not struck down when they confront the target system, and that change, not status quo, may be the outcome.

One notion that runs through all phases of the model is the importance of the joint confrontation, with the client observing and participating in every negotiation and confrontation. While it is important for attorneys to approach the bench, to negotiate outside the courtroom, and to meet privately in judges' chambers, in social work practice it is of paramount significance that the client group be an integral part (at *least* as observers) of every contact with the opposition.

### Phase II: Worker as Organizer-Educator.

This role marks the transition from advocacy and dependence to the beginning of a community development model. The worker now focuses on transmission of knowledge and development of leadership within the client group. The group should have reached the transition between Kurzman's Stage 1 and Stage 2 in terms of their reactions to the *Negeya* bond. The worker recognizes that he must begin to withdraw from the participation-advocacy role, and instead must enable indigenous leadership to become equipped with the skills which have proved effective in achieving group goals.

Certain specific skills must be transferred and certain tasks performed in order to gain these desired ends. The most essential of these include:

*Observation.* The client leaders must be able to share all confrontation experiences with the organizer. For example, in welfare rights organizing, the worker during Phase I should have a client leader or group member present at all advocacy attempts. Gradually, in Phase II, the advocacy responsibility during any such experience must be given to the client-advocate, with the prior preparation and continuing presence of the professional worker.

*Technical Training.* The client group must be prepared for confrontation with the system. Workshops and training classes must be held so that the clients become well versed in the technical data required in the given setting. This may include knowledge of welfare laws and administrative codes, educational policy, housing codes, and so forth. In client confrontations during Phase II, nothing is more upsetting to target system personnel than facing clients who are better versed in their own policies than themselves.

*Role Play.* The use of simulation and role play is extremely helpful in this phase of organization. They are useful in sensitizing client groups to the very real tasks that lie ahead. Further, they provide meaningful tests of leadership as well as an indication of just how far the group has progressed in mastering the technical knowledge required for future confrontations. An additional factor relates to the *Negeya* bond. The client, through staged confrontations with a white professional worker begins to play out his rebellion against the "system." As he liberates himself from the *Negeya*, it becomes easier for him first to confront his worker, whom he has identified as an ally and who seems more like a "native" than a "settler," than to confront the system he has been told to fear. After achieving relative comfort in these training simulations, confronting the system itself is a logical next step in the organizing sequence.

In traditionally black-white settings, the utilization of a white worker to play the role of a white system agent allows the black client a confrontation with a representative of the repressive society. Such a plan seems much closer to reality in this type of setting than in one where a *Negeya* bond exists for other than racial reasons.

Performance during the organizer-educator phase is perhaps the most crucial in attaining a strong, independent group. The worker is tempted to retain his position of control toward the group, which runs counter to the successful completion of Phase II. The demands upon the adaptational skills of the community organization worker are therefore worth noting.

**Phase III: Worker as Organizer-Technical Assistant.**

The worker's role in Phase III is such that his presence is rarely seen by the community-at-large. The group's indigenous leadership is in the forefront, and the organizer assumes various advisory roles which they determine. Transition into Phase III is potentially the most difficult for both worker and client. Both skill and sensitivity are required during this delicate procedure. For in a short period of time, the worker must move (or be moved) out of a position of visible influence and must disengage himself from any residual power he still possesses. In this phase, he begins to serve as a consultant on technical matters, and frequently as an agent for continued leadership development and training within the group.

Here again, the role of the worker is the key to successful organizational maintenance and group cohesion. His role is that of a catalyst rather than an actor, yet he must be cognizant of the group process. His leadership must be the good leadership of Lao Tse: ". . . A leader is where the people hardly know he exists, but a good leader, when the work is done, the aim fulfilled . . . they will say, 'we did this ourselves.' "

## *Experience from Practice*

Illustrations of application of this model may be found in the early history of the Hinds County Welfare Rights Movement. Beginning in May, 1967, the Michael Schwerner

Memorial Fund's Mississippi project engaged in direct advocacy on behalf of welfare recipients as the first phase of a welfare rights organizing effort.

Organizers from the Schwerner Fund's local Community Development Agency, utilizing the same minimum standard requests being accepted by departments of welfare throughout the nation, initiated a massive drive for minimum standards. The Schwerner Fund volunteer organizers consciously took on the roles of leader and advocate for the clients.

As the movement progressed into the summer, Schwerner Fund workers began a training program on welfare laws and on techniques appropriate to challenging the system. The internal structure of the movement gradually crystallized, with indigenous leadership taking the major roles as the program developed. Group training, sensitivity sessions, role play, and significant plenary involvement permitted a great number of clients to learn the techniques of organizing. It was at this juncture that the National Welfare Rights Organization held its first convention. Leaders of the Hinds County movement who attended that convention strengthened their skills and group identity in this setting, and Phase II became an actuality.

Due to the limited time that the volunteers spent in Mississippi, Phase III never had an opportunity to become reality. However, the initial steps were undertaken. Volunteers significantly removed themselves from positions of influence within the movement. Their assistance was primarily that of providing the technical know-how on laws, bureaucracy, and system confrontation. In practice, volunteers found that they met with client groups both prior to and after confrontations. Often, a passer-by would note the volunteers standing across the street from the welfare office, while clients, under their own leadership, met with public welfare officials.

The consultant or technical assistant role described in Phase III is perhaps the most significant part of the model. It meets the need of both client and practitioner. The client, who must break from patterns of dependence, is able to direct his own movements and the future of his organization. Even though it is difficult to remove oneself from the center of a movement, the worker too may find a significant role for himself in consultation and technical assistance.

## Summary

First, we have explored some of the limitations for social work (as an agency-based profession) in embracing the legal model of advocacy. While some of the constraints may be tempered through careful process and practice, other constraints probably would persist unless the profession were to offer an alternative of private practice.

Second, an attempt has been made to reconcile the ideological gap between advocacy and the social work ethic of client self-determination. While social work will continue to borrow from many professions including law, we have concluded that community organization must go *beyond advocacy*, toward a community development model which is consistent with the long-range goals of social work practice.

Three progressive phases of worker intervention are suggested, with practice illustrations of their implementation drawn from the Mississippi experience of the Michael Schwerner Memorial Fund. The ultimate value of this strategy, however, will await its repeated use in a variety of settings by community organization practitioners who are committed to client self-determination and to social change.

## STUDY QUESTIONS

1. Is community organization a legitimate social work function? Is it properly designated a social work method?

2. Is there ever a barrier between professionalism, and productivity and creativity? What is the author trying to say here?

3. Can a profession afford to have members "do their own

thing"? In responding, indicate your understanding of what is meant by "professionalism," and how you would differentiate Movement activity from professional practice.

4. Do you feel the advocacy approach (patterned on the legal model) is appropriate to community organization practice?

5. What are the constraints (if any) of agency auspices upon the social work practitioner? What are some of the advantages (if any) to the worker and client of having an agency auspice?

6. What do you think about Zald's argument for a private practice model for social work? Is it professionally advisable, advantageous? Is it realistically possible, feasible? Explain your answers.

7. What does the author mean when he says (in his discussion of "Sociocare") that the worker would be bound by "client selection and the ethics of the profession, rather than the needs of a social agency"?

8. Do you agree that, where the advocacy model is practiced, client self-determination is difficult to achieve?

9. Do you agree that legal training is better geared to provide confrontation experts than social work training?

10. What is the importance, in Phase I, of achieving early victories—both real and symbolic? Are they ingredients for successful community organization?

11. Do you think the adaptation of the legal-advocate model to Phase I organizing is sound and feasible? Explain. Can you cite any examples from case studies or your practice to substantiate your opinion?

12. In Phase II, why is it so important that clients participate with the organizer in all confrontation experiences?

13. The author suggests that the three most important tasks in Phase II are a) observation, b) technical training, and c) role play. Do you agree with his selection? Are there other tasks you would substitute or add?

14. Role play perhaps most commonly is used as a technique in group work practice. Do you feel it would be helpful

for community organizers to be trained in the use of role play? From your experience, have you found role play a valuable training technique? Discuss.

15. Clearly, the transition from Phase II to Phase III is crucial to the creation of a strong, independent community organization. What are some of the special problems you foresee that might tend to make this transition particularly difficult to achieve? Do you feel that Phase III, as outlined by Solomon, is a realistic expectation?

16. Phase III involves the process of what social workers often term "separation" or "termination." What are some of the problems one should anticipate here? How can the worker prepare the group—and himself—for this crucial experience?

17. Solomon outlines here three phases of community organization. How do these phases differ from Kurzman's three stages of confrontation? How are they similar? Compare and contrast Solomon's three worker roles (organizer-advocate, organizer-educator and organizer-technical assistant) with those suggested by Kurzman (actor-teacher, catalyst-team member and advocate-observer).

18. Does social work education and training prepare a worker with the versatility required to meet the role expectations outlined by the author? Where do you feel social work training is strongest (and weakest) in this regard?

19. Solomon often refers to the activity in Hinds County as "the movement." In a technical sense, what is the difference (if any) between community organization in a social work setting, and community organization in a movement?

20. Do you agree (or disagree) with the author's contention that community organization must go "beyond advocacy" toward a community development model of social work practice? Explain your position.

*PART II*

# MODELS
# FOR PRACTICE

# The Care and Feeding of Southern Welfare Departments

TED SEAVER

It is important to realize that when dealing with southern welfare systems you are faced with a totally reactionary system that is immune from conventional pressure tactics. From the vantage point of the South, the northern big city welfare departments are a utopia of enlightenment and good grants. The average monthly ADC payment in New York is $208.25; in Mississippi, $31.74. In the North there is generally some variety of liberal legislative representation to advocate for the poor. In Mississippi there is none. In the North direct action is a potentially effective pressure tactic. In Mississippi the response, for example, to a sit-in at the welfare office would be immediate and instant arrest with the total and sympathetic approval of the white majority and the legislature, which would probably respond by cutting welfare bene-

From 1965 to 1967, the writer coordinated the Community Development Agency (CDA) in Jackson, Mississippi, which is an action program of the Michael Schwerner Memorial Fund. CDA provided staff services to the county welfare rights movement, and the examples in this paper are drawn from these experiences.

fits. Any regressive trait displayed by northern welfare departments can be found magnified and doubled in the South. Thus the whole context becomes such that to get the welfare department to use "Mr." and "Mrs." with clients becomes a major victory.

The suggestions in this paper are taken from an organizer's experience in a county welfare department in Mississippi. They are not a guaranteed formula, but indicate some of the possible tactics and techniques that can be used to make welfare services slightly more responsive to the needs of the poor. It should be noted that the major issues—inadequate grants and archaic policies—will not be dealt with. The work outlined here rather has three goals: 1) using welfare issues as an organizing device to give people confidence in their ability to negotiate and cope with the system, and an understanding of what creates the system; 2) employing the welfare department's own regulations to pressure for better services; and 3) beginning to create crisis situations that will point out the total inadequacy and internal contradictions of the present welfare system.

## Leverage Points

We found that the worker can exert the most leverage via four tactics:

1. *The Fair Hearing.* Typically, resort to fair hearings in Mississippi has been rare and unusual. We found that the welfare officers dread hearings, because they create a lot of extra work, and are seen as a mark against them. The hearing was one of the few actions that one could use to force the welfare department into a situation where it cost them more time, money and manpower than it would cost the client organization. For example, at a typical hearing we had our client and one representative. The local office had the worker on the case and a supervisor, and the state office had to send a hearing officer and stenographer. After the hearing, they have to make multiple copies of a verbatim transcript of the

proceedings and present the case to the hearing board. Copies also go to the federal Department of Health, Education and Welfare (HEW). By very rough calculation, we estimate that a fair hearing involves at least four welfare department employees in over twenty hours of work while we are expending two to three hours. Of course, this does not count the time of the hearing board itself. Through two months of efforts in conjunction with the NAACP Legal Defense Fund and other organizations, the local county welfare department was forced to add two new hearing officers and expand their office and budget. The effect on the local welfare department, while it may be just psychological, is gratifying in terms of their new willingness to negotiate with a client organization.

2. *HEW.* The possibility of HEW action also is an important tool. A barrage of complaints to HEW will sometimes get at least a telephone call to the local welfare office. Although we are under no grandiose illusions about the possibility of HEW doing anything that will create significant improvement, the psychological effect in getting the local office to negotiate is helpful.

3. *Welfare Regulations.* The county welfare rights organization has a copy of the *Handbook of Mississippi Welfare.* When the local welfare department realizes it is faced with a knowledgeable clientele, the whole atmosphere improves— particularly if a feeling can be generated in the welfare department that the county is crawling with self-taught welfare experts. The most helpful regulations in terms of pressuring the welfare department are the federal regulations requiring a maximum of thirty days for a notice of disposition.

4. *Welfare Workers' Attitudes.* It is important to realize that even while the welfare workers can be committing the most horrendous violations of good practice, their self-defined image is that of "helping the poor." Thus, it is not entirely futile to point out where they are not fulfilling this goal.

How these levers are used largely determines what gains can be made. However, one should know two things. These techniques are not recommended for people whose theory of social change limits them to traditional means; and the victories that are gained must be seen in the light of our goals stated above.

## The Whipsaw or Mau Mau Effect

This technique is effective in Stage 1, when the welfare department's attitude is still one of confident hostility. It is used mainly to open negotiations, although it also may be useful in later stages. The basic dynamic is lever 4, and it is used in conjunction with the "Grave Professional" (see below). In our case, it was used to establish the right to be in the room with the clients while they were being interviewed.

There are two roles—"Mau Mau" and "Moderate." The job of the Mau Mau is to raise the maximum amount of hell in the most militant and annoying way possible. It is functional for the Mau Mau to be totally unprofessional and as offensive as possible. Preferably, he should be a local person or welfare client. The Moderate comes on to the scene later after the uproar has subsided, dripping with sweet reason and terms like "the breakdown of communications" and "what can we do constructively." He should also be sympathetic with the poor beleaguered welfare department that is so understaffed by the cruel legislature. The Moderate takes the attitude that the welfare department is trying to help, and he is there to help them help. The Moderate should also totally ignore the fact that the welfare department can barely conceal their hostility to him, and should appear to take every protestation of good will toward the client on face value.

*Case History 1*: One of the first issues that was raised with the county welfare department was whether or not we could be in the room with the client. At first, the welfare department was ambiguous about this. Finally, we were able to get a letter from the state office, via the NAACP Legal Defense Fund, that it was all right for the client to have somebody with him to give helpful information. On one of our "welfare days" (see "Legal Civil Disobedience" below), armed with the letter, one of our workers took on the Mau Mau role. Since our welfare day overburdened the office, some of the child welfare workers were called downstairs to help with intake. The crisis arose after our organizer corrected one of their workers twice when she misstated policy so that our client would not be eligible. Both times *our* worker (organizer) was right. At this point, one of their supervisors came on the scene. Our worker showed him the letter. The supervisor said that it did not count in this case, and asked her to leave. She then began playing Mau Mau and refused to leave. The supervisor and worker responded by refusing to interview the client. Our worker then left and went to a room where another client was waiting. The welfare supervisor, noting she had disappeared, began telephoning around the building to discover where she was. Finding her, they replayed the whole letter bit, refusing to leave and refusing to interview the client. At this point a policeman, called by the welfare department, appeared on the scene. Our worker decided that going into the rooms was about finished, and settled for talking to various clients. This is a sort of legal misbehavior.

After reporting this back to the Schwerner Fund's project coordinator, the coordinator put on his suit and tie, assumed a most moderate manner, and went to talk to the welfare supervisor. The coordinator half-apologized for the unprofessional manner of our worker, pointing out that the welfare office had not been too professional either; he then expressed professional shock at the presence of the police, wondering what kind of communication breakdown there had been and how we could work it out to the benefit of the client we were both interested in. After some discussion about the overloaded welfare department, how much they were *trying* to do, and the necessity for private interviews so the client would feel comfortable, we got down to the letter—and how we wanted to help (with a little bluffing about federal regulations) by giving information. The upshot of the matter was that since we *could* help them help the client by providing information, and since unfortunately some of the clients had this completely unfounded belief that the welfare was not on their side, it was decided we could be in the room. But if a policy interpretation arose, we should wait until after the interview to tell him, and he would make himself available to us at all times to avoid further communication breakdowns.

## Legal Civil Disobedience

This is primarily a southern tactic to solve the problem of a) the severe penalty for civil disobedience, and b) the local people's general reluctance to demonstrate. It has two purposes: 1) to cause the local welfare department to "flurry"— that is, over-react and display both their inadequacy and hostility (this can result in materials to be used for HEW— see below) ; 2) to create a sense in the local welfare office that they are faced with a well-organized group that can swamp them on a moment's notice, and whom they had better start negotiating with; and 3) to give the client a sense of psychological one-upmanship on the formidable welfare department that earlier seemed able to control him.

The basic concept was developed by a worker in another county. (The dynamics are levers 1, 3 and 4.) He announced throughout the county that on Thursday everyone who had a welfare problem or who wanted to get on welfare should meet at the local welfare office, and that people would be there to help them. On Thursday, over seventy people showed up. According to welfare regulations, an application is made when a client shows up at the welfare office and says that he wants to apply. This begins the thirty-day period. Any case not handled at the end of thirty days automatically can be appealed. This particular worker heightened the effect by requesting 200 appeal forms from the welfare department. Two additional ploys are: 1) Foster in the clients a spirit of good humor. If they get to the point where they are obviously *enjoying* the discomfiture of the welfare office they gain a tremendous psychological advantage. 2) If your group is small, start recruiting other clients that are already there. A great show of taking down names and addresses and consulting over problems should always be made.

*Case History 2*: Instead of the county-wide announcement technique, we substituted specified welfare days, Tuesdays and Thursdays. On our first welfare day we began with only twelve people. However, we began active recruiting among the twenty or so clients already there. Within an hour the atmosphere in the office had changed from the clients apprehensively waiting for the fiat from the white welfare workers to the clients laughing quite openly at the frenzied scurrying and conferences of the workers. The final outcome of this was the establishment of five standing appointments for our clients on Tuesdays and Thursdays, so we would not have to wait all day for service; a complete shift in the interview approach where the interviewers, not knowing whom we had contacted, started making a point of treating people with great tact, carefully explaining the forms, how the budget was figured, and what their rights were. They also stopped using first names; and, while some white workers still cannot bring themselves to say Mr. or Mrs., they avoid the whole use of names rather than use first names. This is a source of quiet enjoyment to the clients, who are fully aware of why they are not using names. Some clients even make a point of cataloguing the techniques used by the worker to avoid the use of courtesy titles.

## The Grave Professional

This is a variation of Mau Mau. Since both Mau Mau and Legal Civil Disobedience have been partially aimed at opening up the welfare office to the point at which they are going to have to deal with the clients; and since the form they feel the most comfortable dealing in is the agency relationship, someone should take on the role of agency head. If the earlier work has been done right, the welfare department should be feeling a strong need to have someone interpret what is going on and help them adjust. It is the job of the Grave Professional to do this.

This person has a dual function: 1) to advocate for the clients and make the welfare department meet their needs; and 2) to give the welfare department the feeling that somebody understands *their* problems and has faith in their capacity to change. It is important for the person playing this role to remember, however, that his advocacy role is his prime one, and that he should not compromise on points for the sake of maintaining his relationship with the welfare department. If he meets an impasse with the welfare department, his tactic should be gentle disagreement until pressures can be built to the point where the welfare department is ready to listen. He should also remember that his role is only a transitional one, and his ultimate aim is to make the welfare department deal directly with a client's organization. The greater part of his prodding should be in this direction. As much as possible, he should include potential client leaders in sessions with the welfare department. Depending on priorities, local talent available, and degree of enlightenment of the welfare department, this role ideally should come to be played by a client.

There are a number of techniques that this person should be aware of to improve his standing with the welfare department:

*The Moderate.* (See Mau Mau above.) Without compromising, a lot of sympathy can be projected toward the welfare department. They *are* understaffed, they do not set policy (although they may secretly approve of it), and they do not determine the grant maximums. Good statements are things like, "It's too bad that some of the clients' hostility toward you is because they blame the welfare department for the lousy grants—it must make working with them difficult." Once the supervisor agrees with this statement, you have accomplished two important things: 1) They admit the clients feel hostile toward them. This is important because it means that if they want to maintain their self-image of *helping* the poor, they are going to have to do something about it. 2) This nudges them in the direction of dealing directly with a client's group, even if their motive is only to explain in order to create policy change.

*"I'm Only Trying to Help You."* This is useful when a disagreement arises between your client's needs and the welfare department. Your response is not to bawl them out, but to sigh mournfully, point out the dreadful possibilities that are vaguely beyond your control, and mention how they can be avoided.

*Case History 3*: At one point, the welfare department reaction to our welfare days was to turn people away by telling them they could not take their applications. We decided that, instead of playing Mau Mau on this, we would use the Grave Professional. We called up and sympathized with the staff shortage, but pointed out that the welfare manual stated that a person's presence in the office requesting assistance constituted an application. We also indicated that since this started the thirty days, it would mean a whole stack of appeals would get filed which would just make life difficult for everyone. After a long discussion about limited budgets, it was decided that they could interview the clients after all, and an appointment was made to discuss ways we could handle cases more efficiently. This later interview led to: 1) a streamlining of the APTD* cases (the clients could go directly to the examining doctor without a preliminary trip to the welfare office); 2) implementing a system by which the welfare office would hold appointment slots for clients referred by our office; 3) the welfare office agreeing to cooperate with our recommendation for training health aides who would be placed in the homes of elderly clients in need of nursing; and, 4) beginning to *think* about the possibility of decentralizing services by placing a worker at one of *our*

---

* Aid to the Permanently and Totally Disabled.

community centers in order to save clients a 70-mile round trip from the rurals. The latter, of course, was so "radical" that it required a lot more thinking.

There are also some ways to pressure the welfare department without destroying your image as the Grave Professional:

*People Make Policy.* This is a comeback against a very well-known welfare department ploy called Run-Around. The essence of your response is based upon the fact that somebody, somewhere, had to make the statement that gets passed on to you as the reason why the welfare department cannot do something. What you have to do (while maintaining a calm professional front) is pin somebody to take responsibility for the statement. This has a marvelously clarifying effect on Run-Around or phony policy statements. One of the most effective ways to implement this technique is to ask whoever makes the statement to put it in writing.

*Case History 4*: On our first appeal, we were faced with the problem of trying to see the clients' records before the actual hearing. Both state and federal regulations were vague on this matter, although the spirit was definitely to let the client see the records. We therefore wrote a letter, signed by the client, authorizing us to examine the records. Armed with a copy of this, we went to the local office. The supervisor, naturally, was not very happy about letting us see the records. After an extended discussion about how they wanted to protect the client from various unscrupulous forces (which we agreed was a good thing), there were a series of hurried conferences and phone calls, the upshot being that they could not give an answer until after lunch. After lunch we returned. "Well," said the supervisor, "the state office says that you cannot see the records until they have a decision from Washington." "When," we asked, "would that be?" Well, they really could not say—they had just been told by the state office that we could not see the records yet. Could they put that in writing? They did not see any reason for *that*. Well, we just thought it would be the most *professional* thing to do so that when we told HEW about it, and for the sake of any lawsuits that might come up, it would be clear exactly who said what and when. We weren't trying to threaten them, were we? Lord, no; we just thought that it was the best kind of professional protection to clarify in writing where policy came from. Well, maybe they had better make some more telephone calls. The final outcome was that we were directed to the state office where we were told that it was certainly all right to look at records and they would be available for us any time prior to a hearing.

*"Status."* Here it is important to remember that southern welfare workers 1) feel that they are not seen by the rest of the country as the most progressive social workers in the world; 2) they think, contrary to reality, that HEW is capable of and willing to radically change the situation; and 3) that "civil rights" workers are endowed with the ability to create major upheavals with the total might of the federal government backing them at a moment's notice. The whole technique in "Status" is to try to reinforce these feelings at every opportunity. At the same time, picture yourself as a reasonable type who will not call in the hounds of HEW except as a last resort. You should emphasize that you believe in using the vast reservoir of good will that lies in the deeply misunderstood South before taking things any further (the last word should be given slightly ominous overtones). At the same time, you should be writing letters like mad and lodging complaints with HEW, Civil Rights Commission, Justice Department, etc., hoping that one of them just might possibly call the welfare office to mention that it wasn't very nice of them not to use courtesy titles. Knowing the name of a member of a compliance team that has recently visited the welfare department is an essential ingredient of Status. You also should familiarize yourself with the names of all bureau chiefs in HEW and drop them from time to time, as in the sentence: "Well, as I told Finch the other day . . ." or, "Of course you're familiar with Winnie Bell's book on ADC where she says . . ." If done correctly, and with the proper

aura of confidence, blatant blunders on the part of the welfare office can be cured immediately, and the groundwork can be laid to effect other changes in the future.

This paper is by no means complete, and it omits some combination and variation techniques. As we continue to care for and feed our local welfare department, we'll probably learn and be forced to use new techniques before we get to the point where we can maintain a games-free relationship. For people who want further instruction and advice on the subject of games, people and institutions, I recommend *Games People Play* and *Gamesmanship*.

## STUDY QUESTIONS

1. In the opening paragraph, Seaver gives us the impression that welfare conditions in the South are quite different from the North. Does this mean, therefore, that one should suspect that techniques and strategies of community organization practice, correspondingly, will be different?

2. It is clear that the client organization's push for fair hearings was very expensive to the state's Department of Social Welfare and the taxpayers. Do you think such a strategy can be defended as an appropriate social work intervention in view of the tremendous cost it brings in terms of staff time and preparation?

3. What is your reaction to the author's frank comment that "these techniques are not recommended for people whose theory of social change limits them to traditional means"?

4. The Mau Mau-Moderate approach underlines the importance of creating conflict and confrontation. Do you feel such deliberate strategies are appropriate? Useful? Professional?

5. Is manipulation a legitimate activity for professional social workers? Does it violate the NASW Code of Ethics? Would you be comfortable with such a model yourself?

6. After reading the first case history: how much of this example seems pertinent to Mississippi, and how much is

characteristic of public welfare systems throughout the country? Would you ever use the same tactics, for example, in New York or Chicago?

7. Social workers traditionally are taught to be "nonjudgmental." How would you reconcile this precept with the principles being suggested in this paper?

8. It is quite clear in the second case history that the organizers were deliberately attempting to make the welfare workers look inept and foolish in the eyes of their clients. Why were they eager to do this? What are the advantages in terms of the ultimate goals of the welfare rights movement? Do you feel such an approach is valid?

9. Contrast the worker's approach in Case Histories 1 and 3. When would you use the Mau Mau-Moderate approach; when would the Grave Professional be likely to be more useful? Can you cite parallel examples of when you might have used these strategies in your own practice? Do you think these strategies would have been more or less effective than those you chose at that time? Why?

10. In Case History 4, the worker deliberately threatens and/or "blackmails" the welfare agent in his references to lawsuits and HEW. Can such an approach be justified in terms of the worker's goals and the unmet needs of the clients? Explain.

11. There clearly is a quality of condescension implicit in the material presented by Seaver, and in the article's title. What are your personal and professional reactions?

12. Do you feel that conflict can be functional? Do you feel that a "gaming" strategy is appropriate and helpful? What are some of the implications in this regard for social work training and practice?

# The Conscious Use of Color: Some Attitudes and Roles for the White Worker

Barbara A. Schram

There has been much discussion in the last few years of the civil rights movement about the negative effects of using white workers in the "black revolution." After years of subservience to white leadership, it is not surprising that in reaction, current thinking among many dedicated workers, both black and white, leads them to feel that the white worker has no place left in the movement.

The pattern evident in the civil rights movement has obvious and immediate relevance for the field of social work. For here, too, there is a growing realization that the social work establishment has tended to mirror and reinforce the prevailing caste system in society: the black client as follower, the white worker as leader. White workers, even those with the best intentions, have fallen into the "leader role" because they have not been conscious of the typical response their presence evokes in a setting of poor black persons. Social workers have tended to brush aside race as a significant variable, not realizing that it permeates every facet of a relationship in our society. It is the premise of this paper that the ethnicity of the worker is a variable that must be not only constantly identified, but also consciously used.

It does seem evident that the whole area of the white social worker organizing primarily black clients needs a good deal of scrutiny. We do not feel the question is one of should they "stay" or "leave." Rather, how can white workers use themselves so that their race and class, with all they imply, support and supplement the efforts of the poor? We will attempt to delineate roles that the white worker can take on to support the effort of low-income blacks to organize. Many of these roles will be unique to a white worker.

The Deep South setting—with its stark clarity of relationships between black and white—offers "ideal-type concepts" which, with appropriate variations, may be applicable in other areas of the country. Most of the examples in this paper are drawn from the welfare rights setting in Mississippi.

## *Attitudinal Prerequisites*

Before enumerating the specific tasks that a white worker can perform, one must point out the emotional and intellectual set that the white worker must bring to his job of helping the black poor organize themselves to change societal institutions. On the most basic level, the white worker must accept the postulate that, since Reconstruction, the black citizen has continued to be systematically excluded from the economic and political power structures of the country. The worker must recognize that the South represents an archetype of colonial society in which all the decisions that affect the life of the black citizen are made by a privileged white élite. This élite has maintained control over the black man through the use of sanctioned force, both economic and physical, as well as through an ongoing process of brainwashing that propels an image of the black as being "less than a man," inferior by nature of heredity and "natural law." This belief in the non-equality of the black man has been used by the white Southerner to rationalize his own monopoly of the political system and, in turn, has often come to be accepted by the black man himself. As long as the black man accepts the white man's image of him he is trapped in a vicious circle of self-hatred and poverty. His only hope of changing the traditional system of the South is to break out of this long condition of self-denigration and then organize to wrest power away from the privileged élite.

It is vital that the white worker study the history and sociology of racism so that he can intellectually grasp the enormity of the problem. But intellectual insight is obviously not enough. The emotional set of the worker must take preeminence. He must, in effect, reject many of the beliefs and methods of the white world. As he comes to understand the dimension of the problem and commits himself to changing his own world, he will inevitably experience enormous anger, frustration and even hate. At the same time, he will discover that even with great effort he can never experience the total sense of powerlessness felt by a poor black man in the South.

In many ways, traditional social work maxims only hamper the worker as he tries to come to grips with intense emotional feelings. The stances of "objectivity," "nonjudgmentalness," and "mediation" actually may prove dysfunctional as the worker struggles to get as close as possible to the people's feelings of despair and fear (as well as his own feelings of rage at the injustice he sees all around him). In a situation in which poor people are starving daily, it becomes patently clear that a system that condones this must be confronted with any weapon that will work. "Judgment" may be necessary when a system is evil and corrupt; "mediation" may not be possible when the poor have no options; and "objectivity" cannot bring a white worker to the emotional understanding he needs to function in this setting.

## The "Employee" Set

The white worker must be clear to himself and his clients that he is there to work *at their direction.*

The term "client" connotes a subordinate set in the minds of most social workers. It is imperative that the worker redefine the client-worker relationship so that he becomes an employee of the black community. It is imperative that the white worker avoid falling into a dominant role with black clients. It is of no ultimate gain for them to exchange a punitive "boss man" for a benevolent one. The worker should act to help his clients gain vitally needed services, but only in a way that will help them build their own sense of power and dignity as well as their own skills in negotiating with the white world. Striking a balance in which the white worker can act as informal consultant without offending or frightening clients by too much unexpected familiarity should be the conscious effort.

To be fully committed to the client as employer—rather than to an agency or profession—is flying in the face of tradition. It is also precarious, for the white worker in a black movement accepts a position of marginality in which he does not have (or seek) full membership in either the black or the white community.

## 1. The Worker as Technical Consultant.

As the black man has been excluded systematically from power positions in the systems that affect his life, whites have been able to keep from him relevant information and skills that one must have if he is to confront these systems and change them. In his role of technical consultant, the worker's most obvious and immediate function is to make available to his clients knowledge about the system they are planning to engage. The worker takes on responsibility for researching appropriate laws and other written documents and digesting them into a form that can be used readily by people unaccustomed to dealing with this type of material. For example, within welfare law there are overlapping federal, state and county welfare regulations that must be sorted out and identified. The worker who began the organizing of the welfare rights movement in Hinds County had to begin by acquainting welfare clients with their legal right to a fair hearing, how to file, what the legal requirements of the hearing were, and how they could get the most from the actual hearing process. Although the clients' right to a fair hearing is supposed to be explained by each welfare intake worker, not one request had been filed in Hinds County until the emergence of the welfare rights movement.

Acting on the expressed priorities of his clients, the worker assumes a responsibility for information gathering and interpreting. Although this function obviously can be filled by either a white or a black worker familiar with handling the paraphernalia of the bureaucratic world, the white worker frequently finds greater accessibility to information. Often he can more easily establish the informal contacts with white officials that lead him most quickly to obtaining the most valuable inside information. The "cover" of white skin can often open up the doors to records and materials that might well be closed to a black person, lay or professional.

It might seem from what we say that the worker will have to be a walking encyclopedia of welfare law and practice. This is not necessarily so. By sheer knowledge of the middle-class way of doing things, whites have a great deal of valuable information to contribute. The worker can see intuitively the tactics that "his system" uses and is thus able to begin providing the information that clients need in order to "play the game better."

For example, when working on a food stamp program, it was found that information most beneficial to the client was a definition of what constitutes proof of an expense. It was readily apparent from witnessing a couple of interviews that welfare workers used the issue of proof to intimidate the client so that he would not claim all his expenses, thereby making grants smaller. They did advise clients that they had to prove their expenses by bringing in bills and receipts. They would accept handwritten notes from landlords as proofs of rent, but did not advise clients that notes from other creditors, such as the man who hauls water or who drives the client to work, also would be acceptable. Clients do not usually receive receipts for the money spent for such services. Consequently, the issue of whether transportation or water hauling expenses were deductible never arose.

With this attitude on the part of the food stamp worker, it is no wonder that the client never really comprehends the game, never really learns how to work within the system to his own best advantage. It is the white worker's first job to make available to the clients knowledge of their rights, *and* to begin to instill the attitude of game playing. For the clients, so long policed by the welfare and food stamp workers, have from necessity adopted a docile and obedient demeanor. Consequently, they will not bring in a bill on the chance that it may be deductible—they do as they are told, i.e., they bring in proof when the welfare worker tells them to and only for expenses that they are *told* to prove. Opening up the possibilities and encouraging initiative can be done by the white worker with little knowledge of the particulars of the law.

In his role of "technical consultant" the worker also can draw together and put in usable form materials published by other groups that have relevance to members. Mimeographed papers and pamphlets put out by small groups, especially in the South, constitute a wide literature of experience. In a similar fashion, the worker may be the only person available who has the technical ability to record the experiences of the group and disseminate them further. Moreover, additions to the social work literature, phrased in the language and style of academia, can help narrow the widening gap between clients, community organization practitioners, and the schools of social work.

## 2. The Worker as Decoder.

The isolation of the black poor from the seats of power and decision-making has not only kept welfare clients from the basic knowledge of their legal rights and the methods of protest, but further has kept them from understanding the cues one needs to know in order to successfully interact with the welfare system. The black client must begin to learn the hidden agendas of the welfare agents if he is to successfully handle his dealings with them. While the welfare client has often doubted the sincerity and integrity of the welfare agents, he has never been given the reassurance or evidence that his questioning is valid.

For example, many potential welfare recipients are fearful of applying for AFDC (Aid to Families with Dependent Children) because of a document they must sign which gives the courts the right to sue the putative father for support. The welfare agents call this a "paper against the father" and warn clients that the father will be "locked up" if he does not provide support. While this may be technically true, in actual practice the State of Mississippi is hardly equipped to track down every wandering male. In addition to not having the resources to do this, they are well aware that, even if they were to locate the father, he would probably not be making enough money to substantially add to the support of the family. The worker shares this "how it really is" with the client so that she can have a more accurate and balanced picture of what may happen if she signs. In the same vein, the welfare agents warn mothers of out-of-wedlock children that they can be prosecuted for adultery and their children taken away if they admit to their "crime" in signing a request for welfare. In actual fact, the State of Mississippi cannot adequately place the large number of black foundling children it already has on its caseloads and would much rather have the mother take care of these children than have her in prison with the children as wards of the state. What the welfare agent is doing by keeping from the clients the actual *practice* of the law is attempting to keep down her caseload by scaring off the most timid of her clients. Since Mississippi welfare grants go to the brave and persistent, the organizer can expose the hidden agendas so that *his* clients can make a decision based upon facts and experience.

The worker is needed not only to decode the system for

the client, but also to decode the complicated language and behavior of the welfare agents. It is valuable service for the worker simply to translate what the welfare agent is saying into direct expression. For example, after a meeting with the county agent (the supervisor of a welfare department) the worker sat with clients and decoded what the phrase "we would like to do this but regulations don't permit it" really means; or, what "we will certainly study this problem" means. The significance and purpose of the agent's behavior were discussed; i.e., overpoliteness (I'm a good-guy), providing chairs for all members of the client group who had come to complain (divide and conquer), the lengthy introductory monologue by the agent (taking control of the situation) and such debating tactics as "of course you will agree that . . ." The white middle-class world has long intimidated the poor through the use of language and jargon; the white worker therefore *translates* for his clients the terms used by "his world."

The worker—and especially the white worker—can often quickly see through the personality set of the white welfare agent. It is, for example, endemic to most Mississippi welfare agents that they need to maintain the illusion that they are "helping people." It would damage their need to feel like professional social workers if they were to face the realities of the system in which they operate. Welfare agents often hesitate, for example, to call the police to handle an altercation with a client because this would then explode the myth of their being able to work professionally with people. Welfare clients who realize this, with some degree of impunity can stage a demonstration in a welfare department that would get them all arrested and brutally handled if they were to act similarly at a courthouse or a commercial establishment.

It is vital that the white worker constantly point out the fallibilities of welfare agents and encourage black people to express their feelings of dislike, scorn and ridicule. As the white worker sanctions and encourages discussions of the inadequacies of the welfare agents as practitioners and as people, the black man begins to feel that he need no longer blame himself and his neighbors for his predicament, but can begin to blame the white man's systems instead. Chipping away at the black man's self-hate and self-denigration by focusing the anger where it justly belongs is more easily accomplished by a white worker. Because of the worker's whiteness (and the authority that accompanies this condition) his sanctioning of the criticism of and anger at the white world is very effective. It is only as the black breaks out of his feelings that "white is right" that he can begin to challenge the power the white man wields.

The model is perhaps that of the *turncoat*: one who goes into the enemy camp armed with a vast supply of knowledge of his own side's culture which he offers to the opposing side to use as a part of their arsenal of weapons. In this setting, the white worker has defected from the white world and is giving the black community the benefit of his inside information. While professionals may cringe from such a model, it has useful implications. The black people of Mississippi are, in fact, fighting for the barest elements of sustenance while the Mississippi welfare system is committed to withholding as much as (and often more than) the law permits. In a situation where a system offers, grudgingly and to only the most persistent, a welfare allocation of *27 per cent of need*, the battle for survival and change must be sharply pitched.

### 3. The Worker as Dry-Run White.

The two roles we have just outlined involve the actual transmitting of information and skills to black clients which will enable them to more effectively deal with the system. While information, both implicit and explicit, is vital for the black welfare client, his ability to use these insights in a direct confrontation with a white is a tremendously difficult step. While no practice situation can ever re-create the fear present in a real-life welfare interview, the white organizer can use himself as the object to be practiced upon.

In meetings held before major confrontations, a white welfare rights worker would assume the role of the anticipated adversary, evoking responses from black clients. On many occasions, the fact that it was a role play would begin to be lost and the black client would begin to humble himself as he would in ordinary encounters. At this point, the audience was encouraged to discuss what was happening. Then the scene would be replayed—over and over again—with excitement mounting and the premium being placed on "winning" the encounter. The very words used and the gestures made were new experiences for most black clients; and, as the actors lost themselves in the encounter, they found themselves saying things to a white they would not have dared to say before.

While there are many risks for the black man in directly confronting a white, as the movement begins to grow and the stories of triumphs are shared a kind of buoyancy and strength begins to be shared among clients. While the white worker must always point out the consequences that may occur when one directly confronts the power structure, clients begin to develop both the skills and the psychological set which open up this new option of confrontation.

In addition to the practice of role play, it is functional for the worker to get into genuine disagreements with his clients and encourage them to fight back. When this happens, black clients develop a greater potential to face the outside world of hostile whites. If they can confront their white worker they can begin to speak directly to others who have the same "magical color" and "fancy speech."

## 4. The Worker as Intervener with the White World.

The "intervener role" must be used with the greatest amount of caution as it brings the white worker into face-to-face relationships with the white establishment. Here the worker must be particularly alert to the possibility that he may end up increasing his *own* power vis-à-vis the white community without adding to the skill and power potential of his black clients. Although the white worker involved with the welfare rights movement is seen as an outside agitator who "does not fully understand the situation," white officials still would rather negotiate with him than face an encounter with their own clients. At the beginning of an organizing venture the black people themselves may fear encounters with the white establishment and may be more comfortable having "their white worker" speak out on their behalf.

In addition to the pressures to become a broker or mediator (exerted by both the system and clients), the social worker tends to propel himself into this role—essentially the role his profession has prepared him for and hence what his programmed reactions dictate. While it protects the client against the wrath of the system, white worker intervention may produce results quickly in situations of enormous deprivation. The worker knows that a group needs success, especially at the beginning, and he is aware that his negotiations could bring about at least minor triumphs. But ultimately, the white worker must be aware that his use of the broker role can play into the hands of the white system, as it keeps the black client in a dependent role.

There are several devices open to the white worker which may permit him to help his clients achieve needed successes without increasing his own power. His position as employee of the black clients is most significant. His words and acts must constantly reinforce this to the blacks as well as to the white welfare workers. Even when alone with white officials, he must constantly reiterate that he cannot commit the organization to any course of action until he has checked with the members. He can even leave a meeting, make a phone call and return with an answer that they have agreed to meet and discuss the issue at hand. While the worker may imply that he might have some influence (which legitimizes him with the white community), he must force the officials to refer back to the organization of which he is only an employee.

Similarly, in instances in which the worker is with his

clients at a public meeting, he must develop a set of physical as well as verbal techniques to keep the interaction from flowing between whites. While at the meeting, he may address his client at several points and ask her to answer questions addressed to himself, saying: "Mrs. X knows more about that than I could" or, "Mrs. X and I must discuss this before any action can be taken." In certain encounters he may speak only to his client, never speaking directly to the white official, to clearly point out that he has no relationship whatever with anyone at the conference but the client that he serves.

In the context of these devices and cautions we can begin to delineate some specific ways the worker can use himself in various encounters:

*The Professional Image.* The white worker, dressed in "city clothes," bearing the stamp of his education and training, and consciously using his "social-workese," can often provoke racist white workers into dealing with clients in a more self-conscious manner. By frequent allusions to the "professional role," welfare agents often are forced to take positions that they would not assume if they were dealing with a client alone.

A traditional stance of the white organizer in the Mississippi Project was to start an interview with a welfare agent by reassuring her that what the client had reported could not possibly be true because no professional would commit such an act! While resulting changes in the worker's behavior cannot hope to be long-range, the client may experience an immediate gratification of his requests which will encourage him to join the welfare rights movement. It can also give the client the knowledge that the welfare agent *can* act differently toward him. After the client has experienced being treated with some level of dignity, he will be far less likely to accept second-class treatment again, and is encouraged to develop his own techniques to evoke better service.

By his very presence, the professional at the side of the client can force doubts into the mind of the white welfare agent. While the welfare agent can dismiss the sandaled college student as a beatnik agitator, it is far more difficult to write off the professional who quotes Gordon Hamilton. The committed bigot cannot be reached on this level, but the borderline liberal often begins to raise some questions about his agency and the system it is perpetuating. Any gnawing doubts that may exist can be exacerbated and should be consciously played upon.

*The Shield.* This role, similar to the professional image, plays upon the system's fear of exposure to the outside world. The worker's main assets are his professionalism and his whiteness. In one instance in Mississippi, for example, a white, northern sociologist teaching at a local college came with his students to do "research" on a boycott and picket run by black people. His taking of notes and pictures was a guarantee to the participants that the most obvious episodes of police brutality would be avoided, and he was accepted by the police because he was seen as academically neutral. A stenographer (especially a white one) taking notes at a meeting likewise has a salutary effect.

## The Use of the White Worker Over Time

The uses of the professional white worker in a rights movement are fluid and should change through time. Additionally, the need for him should obviously vary according to the current state of the movement, its period of organization, its task and its milieu. Movements change throughout their organizational life, and roles that are appropriate during early phases, later (in a more organized period) can become dysfunctional and hold a movement back.

As we view the continuum of organizing stages, we believe the first roles to be dropped are the intervention ones. As the clients' knowledge and skills develop, the worker should relinquish those roles which the clients are ready to take on. Eventually, the worker's role will diminish to that of solely a technical consultant, working on an "as needed" basis at the request of the indigenous leadership. If the worker has performed his functions skillfully, when time for disaffiliation comes, the leadership of the group itself should be ready and able to eject him.

Clearly, the white worker is best utilized in the beginning phases of the movement. It is in the initial upsetting of the traditional roles between black and white that the worker's whiteness can be used so well. When the white community begins to deal directly with the indigenous leadership, the skin color of the white worker is no longer necessary as a tool. At this point it is probably most beneficial for a black professional to fill the position. Eventually, of course, the indigenous leadership must take over the majority of the functions of any professional worker.

It must be recognized that this disaffiliation can be a very painful process for the worker who has invested so much of himself in the group. The pangs of separation can be acute when the group you have nurtured, survived battles with, established warm friendships within, and are identified with —through the assertion of its *own* will—in essence rejects you. It is all too easy for the worker's feelings to influence his professional judgment at this juncture, so great care and soul-searching must accompany the worker's reactions. The worker can take consolation in the fact that the *achievement* of this phase is a sign of his job well done.

## Summary: The Conscious Use of Skin

The unique feature of the white worker is his whiteness. The patterns of interaction between the races have been set by tradition. It is through the conscious use of his whiteness that the worker can help change the quality of the interaction, and obliterate the traditional roles of dominant and subservient.

In effect, the white worker is lending the aura of his color to the black client—lending him its protection and its power to evoke certain types of responses from the white community. But whiteness is used not only to break down the traditional responses of the white community to the black, but also to change the traditional response of black to white. When the worker lends the black client his whiteness, he also lends a self-image, a mental posture, and a consequent set of role expectations which may be foreign to the client role.

Certainly much of the content of the work—the procuring of information, technical consultation, strategy planning, etc. —can be accomplished by a trained black worker. The use of the white worker is really an expedient. It immediately throws the traditional roles into sharp contrast, and, through role reversal (turncoat to the white community and dry-run white with the black community), hastens the process of change.

## The Relevance of These Experiences to Organizing in General

Although we have focused on the use of the worker's whiteness, we have discussed attitudes and techniques that can be applied in other situations. There are some generalizations that can be made from what we have learned working with the movement in Mississippi to organizing with any client, anywhere.

We have found that the emotional and intellectual set which we specified as necessary for work with the Mississippi black community is just as necessary elsewhere. It is important for the worker in any community to realize that not only the blacks but the poor in general have been systematically excluded from rising in the economic and social system. North as well as South, they are victims rather than perpetrators of poverty.

The employee relationship that the worker assumes toward his clients is of importance North as well as South with whites as well as blacks, for it functions to break down the traditional caste roles and to develop client leadership and initiative. Where we are not trying to mitigate the effects of the *caste* system, we are trying to mitigate the effects of the *class* system.

These findings then become not just a prescription for organizers in the South with the black community, but a general statement of social work philosophy for organizing the disadvantaged or those overwhelmed by *any* of the repressive institutions in our society.

STUDY QUESTIONS

1. Do you agree with the author that "race permeates every facet of a relationship" in our society? Discuss.

2. Do you agree with Schram that the question today is not whether white workers should stay in the black community or leave—but rather, how they use themselves in this setting?

3. How important do you feel study of history and sociology of racism to be as a prerequisite for the white worker in the black community?

4. The author suggests that traditional stances of "objectivity," "nonjudgmentalness" and "mediation" may prove dysfunctional for the white worker in the black community. Do you agree or disagree? Explain your position.

5. What are some of the strengths (and limitations) of redefining the client-worker relationship as the author proposes? Do you think the redefinition is workable, realistic?

6. The author implies that the white worker, as a member of the middle class and its oppressive, bureaucratic systems, is in a unique position to interpret these systems to the black community. Do you agree? Do you feel this is a legitimate, professional function?

7. What is really meant by the term "the worker as decoder"? What are the "codes" referred to?

8. Schram says, ". . . it would damage the [Mississippi welfare agents'] need to feel like professional social workers if they were to face the realities of the system in which they

operate." Do you agree? Explain your answer. Could this be true for workers in the North as well?

9. Do you think it is ethical (and professional) for the white worker to encourage discussion among clients of the inadequacies of the welfare agents "as practitioners and people"? Defend your position.

10. The author characterizes her decoder concept as a model of the worker as "turncoat," offering the black community an arsenal of weapons to fight the system. Do you feel this role is appropriate, given the worker's responsibilities to his agency, his peers and his profession? Is such a stance consistent with our Code of Ethics?

11. Discuss some of the advantages and limitations of role play in this setting.

12. The pressures for the white worker to become a "broker" or a "mediator" are referred to, and rejected. Explain these two social work roles as you understand them, and indicate whether you agree or disagree with the writer about their effectiveness in this setting.

13. Schram refers to the worker's need to develop a set of "physical as well as verbal techniques" to keep the interaction at formal meetings from flowing between whites. What does she mean to imply by the term "physical techniques"? What is the role of nonverbal communication in social work practice?

14. "While the welfare agent can dismiss the sandaled college student as a beatnik agitator, it is far more difficult to write off the professional who quotes Gordon Hamilton." Discuss.

15. Which of the four new roles for the white worker do you find most useful, helpful? Why? Correspondingly, which do you find least useful? Why?

16. The writer says, "the white worker is best utilized in the beginning phases of the movement." Do you agree?

17. "Whiteness is used not only to break down the traditional responses of the white community to the black, but

also to change the traditional responses of black to white." Do you agree with this proposition? Are both goals valid?

18. In discussing the relevance of this paper to community organizing in general, the author states: "Where we are not trying to mitigate the effects of the *caste* system, we are trying to mitigate the effects of the *class* system." What are some of the implications of this statement?

# Welfare Rights
## as Organizing Vehicle

RONALD M. ARUNDELL

> Is it not much better to even die fighting for something
> than to have lived an uneventful life, never gotten any-
> thing and leaving conditions the same or worse than
> they were and to have future generations go through the
> same misery and poverty and degradation? The only
> people whose names are recorded in history are those
> who did something. The peaceful and indifferent are
> forgotten; they never know the fighting joy of living.
> —ELIZABETH GURLEY FLYNN

With the cry "More money now!" thousands of welfare
recipients are beginning to rise and fight the oppression of
the welfare system. In city after city they have organized
into Welfare Rights Organizations. Using the various techniques of the civil rights movement, they have struggled to
gain minimum standards, the implementation of fair hearing
appeals, collective bargaining, and special grants for emergency situations. Clients who were once passive and apathetic
have now rebelled. They demand "bread, dignity, justice,
and a better life for their families."

The first section of this paper will deal with the steps followed in establishing a welfare rights organization; the second will explore the various phases that seem to exist in welfare rights organizing; the third will seek to examine the differences that exist between organizing welfare clients in the North and in the South.

## Why Welfare Rights?

In 1964, the Community Development Agency (CDA) was organized under the sponsorship of the Michael Schwerner Memorial Fund in Jackson, Mississippi.

CDA has operated primarily in Hinds County which has an approximate population of 250,000 people, 60 per cent white and 40 per cent black. CDA has focused on the growth and development of the 100,000 oppressed members of the Hinds County black community, providing technical assistance to local community organizations, assisting groups in drawing up OEO proposals, organizing voter registration, and assisting black farmers in gaining their cotton allotments. It also has worked with welfare recipients.

In Hinds County, where the median income ranks second in the state at $4,783, there are 13,207 public assistance recipients, the largest number of recipients of all eighty-two counties in Mississippi. The county is industrialized in comparison to the rest of the state; nonetheless, agriculture is still an important factor in the economic life of the area.

Through their involvement in various civil rights activities, the CDA staff came into contact with a significant number of black people who were experiencing trials and inconveniences with the welfare system. Moreover, these welfare recipients found it difficult to relate to organizations that in no way served their specific needs. What resulted was a tendency on the part of these welfare clients to remain aloof from the civil rights movement out of fear or shame. Therefore, a significant section of the black community remained unorganized. The staff of CDA realized that some organization which related to the specific needs of this group was urgently needed. Since welfare organizing was going on across the nation, it was decided that a welfare rights organizing campaign would be attempted.

There were other reasons for beginning an organizing effort in welfare. This type of organizing would offer a channel of involvement to a large number of blacks who had never before been involved in any type of group effort. It would give to a disenfranchised people a vehicle whereby they could not only achieve local goals, but also relate to the larger struggle of black people around them for freedom, justice, and equality.

Secondly, welfare organizing would facilitate voter registration. Welfare rights groups established by welfare clients in their own neighborhoods provide a base for organizational operation and an effective communication system for registration and voting drives. The welfare organization would also assist black candidates because there would be a visible constituent structure to which they could relate.

Furthermore, welfare rights organizing would offer a viable way to attack the discriminatory hospital situation, the hunger problem, and the lack of social services for black people. Welfare clients were exploited in areas of health, food, and social services. By organizing the clients into a strong bloc, some of these social systems could be attacked and changed, whereas confrontation by the individual client would in no way be effective.

As important as the above reasons is the fact that welfare organizing develops in the recipient new role models and therefore helps him to grow as a person. Bernard Diamond, a psychoanalyst, remarks that the welfare system mirrors the conflicts of our society with primitive emotions and fears. He maintains the emotions are love and hate. The society simultaneously loves and hates its poor, its dependent, and its disabled. The emotion of love requires that the poor and weak be protected, nurtured, and provided for, as if they were helpless children. Failure to do so would cause collective guilt which would prevent those who have from enjoying what they have, knowing that others have not. Our love for the poor arises out of guilt rather than compassion. Our acts of charity both as individuals and as the collective family of the state are thus primarily for our benefit rather than for the benefit of the recipient. Thus the welfare programs are designed to safeguard health, safety, morals, and well-being of the fortunate rather than directly to improve the lot of the unfortunate.

It is not surprising, therefore, that welfare recipients are treated as nonpersons—sharply cut off from the major benefits to be derived from the society. Particularly, the nonperson (the client) is not allowed the privilege of having a say over his own destiny or that of the society in which he lives. He is not removed from the society, but rather is retained, cared for, and nurtured.

Every encounter by the welfare recipient becomes a reinforcement that he is worth nothing as a human being. Every time he enters the welfare center, he realizes that he is unimportant. The system is structured to keep the recipient in his place. In the hospital, in his home, at the store, with his friends, the system never lets the recipient forget he is worthless.

The importance of welfare organizing lies in *its ability to change this relationship between the recipient and the system*. Every time, with his Welfare Rights Organization, a client pickets, sits-in, fights for his friend, or wins money to which he is entitled, his role changes from one who bears oppression, to one who fights oppression. By seeking a confrontation with the enemy (the welfare department) the nonperson as a member of a WRO forces the system to negotiate with him as a person: collective bargaining requires two equals, two human beings. Hence, every tactic and every confrontation with the welfare department is geared to blasting the bonds of servitude.

It is for these reasons, then, that welfare rights was chosen as an organizing vehicle in Mississippi. For it is here that one sees most easily the failures of the American system. Mississippi is a microcosm of the whole country.

## Background

The climate in Hinds County was excellent for welfare organizing. For a number of years the black people had been involved in voter registration drives, boycotts, a freedom school, Head Start programs under the Child Development Group of Mississippi (CDGM), integration of public facilities, and freedom rides. Moreover, there was a strong black leadership cadre composed of businessmen, clergy, and civil rights organizers.

A year earlier, the Hinds County Community Council had been established. The Council attempted to solidify the gains that had been made during the hectic years of activity from 1963 to 1966. They were able to assist residents to attain their proper cotton allotments and register to vote, train local black political candidates in their quest for office, provide assistance for Head Start programs, and assist the community in poverty board elections. Moreover, HCCC was instrumental in beginning to develop a skilled group of indigenous organizers in many areas of the county.

Added to this were active lawyers' groups such as the NAACP Legal Defense Fund, the Lawyers' Constitutional Defense Committee (LCDC), and the President's Committee for Civil Rights Under Law. These organizations were well known and well respected. They also had some experience in welfare law and had handled many cases.

This history of organizing made it easier for outside organizers to establish rapport in Hinds County. The new workers did not have to start from the beginning; they could utilize the existing structures established by the Hinds County Community Council and other civil rights organizations.

## The Early Experience

On arriving in Jackson, the new organizers established contact with the liberal leadership in the county. A series of meetings were arranged with various ministers, the president of the Mississippi Freedom Democratic Party (MFDP), the editor of the *Mississippi Newsletter,* lawyers, and civil rights organizers.

At these meetings, the purposes and history of the welfare rights movement were explained, while the strategy that the organizers hoped to initiate was outlined. The meetings served to acquaint these persons with the structure of the welfare system and the means whereby organization could begin to remove abuses. The knowledge of the welfare structure and laws had been minimal for most of the leaders. This fact had been observed by most welfare organizers throughout the country and thus was no surprise. One important function of the welfare rights movement has been to educate community leaders on the welfare system and its abuses. While some leaders were skeptical as to the success of this effort, approval and support were given.

After consultation with the leadership, contact was made in the local communities. Using the existing structure of the HCCC, the welfare organizers began to contact local leaders and explain the welfare rights movement. Then these local leaders would set up meetings in their areas at which one of the organizers would be present to explain the movement.

Each evening a different group would be visited. The standard procedure was to meet at a home or church and have the clients fill out minimum standard forms. The organizer would explain the form as the clients were working on it. After all the forms were completed a down-to-earth discussion about welfare law would begin. As the worker explained the law, the clients became aware of how their rights were being violated. The meeting would finish with the group usually expressing a desire to join the welfare rights organization. A time would be set for the following morning to drive people to the county welfare office, either to apply for assistance, or to have their present checks adjusted.

The procedure of meeting in the evening followed by a visit to the welfare center in the morning was repeated throughout the summer. This served to build the groups by meeting their immediate needs, while at the same time preparing them for future independent action against the welfare department. The value of going to the welfare center *with* the clients was to acquaint them with a new role model. Each time a group would go to the welfare department they would be prepared beforehand. They would go in as a group and leave as a group. The worker would sit with the clients and constantly harass the investigators. This was done in order to have the clients experience the vulnerability of the investigator. Whenever workers entered the center or had contact with welfare officials it was usually conflict orientated. In order to be successful it was important that the clients begin to see the system for what it was: the enemy.

The clients began to experience a new phenomenon. The welfare department officials were afraid of *them*. Caught off guard by group effort and the technical knowledge of the organizers, the officials began to look foolish. They stuttered, lost tempers, became excessively polite, and finally would begin to grant group demands. And with each new concession, a new demand was made.

During the month of June it was decided that a mass rally would be a useful tool to put the welfare movement on a strong footing. On June 30, 1967, three weeks after the initial contacts with clients had been made, a rally and march were held. By this time momentum had been built sufficiently so that the demonstration at the Hinds County Welfare Department proved very effective. The rally was held at a downtown church with 200 people present from all over the county. They were black and they were welfare recipients. The president of the MFDP and the candidate for state representative addressed the group. Both were influential black leaders whose presence provided prestige to the occasion. For the first time in their lives, welfare clients were considered important enough to be addressed by community leaders.

As they marched through Jackson with their signs, one could feel the solidarity that developed. Each person then presented his basic need form to the county welfare agent.

Her expression of amazement at such an "insurrection" provided the people with an important experience. She was
truly scared. "Imagine," one client related later, "she couldn't
talk right. We sure showed her." The system was being confronted; nonpersons were forcing the system to see them as
people.

Word spread throughout the county and state, and calls
from all over requesting information about the Hinds County
Welfare Rights Movement gave the organizers all they could
do to get to meetings. As new organizers came to Jackson,
their time was divided between the eight original groups
formed before the June march, and the new groups that had
to be formed. The original groups held weekly meetings at
which the mechanics of establishing a local welfare group
were discussed along with welfare law. Role playing was
used as a teaching device. Officers were elected and dues col-
lected. A structure began to develop.

Slowly, a leadership core began to emerge, and it was
decided that a special effort would be made to concentrate
on the development of this leadership group. Because most of
the organizers would be in the area only for the summer, it
would be necessary to leave an experienced cadre that would
be able to carry on the work of the organization.

While continuing other efforts, regular training sessions
were held for the Executive Committee of the Hinds County
Welfare Rights Organization, which consisted of two members
elected by each local group. Their responsibility was to
coordinate their local (neighborhood) activities and to assist
in planning county-wide actions. This group also served as
a communication link between groups. Such a structure
allowed local groups to suggest ideas, and also enabled ideas
to flow horizontally from one group to another.

At the training sessions, welfare law, social services, and
organizing tactics were discussed, and various confrontations
with the system were planned: a sit-in at the office of the
State Commissioner of Welfare, a meeting with the county
welfare agent, and a statewide welfare workshop. In addition, the Executive Committee assisted the NAACP with

their March on Jackson and negotiated with Head Start to have community workers drive recipients to the welfare office. Two members of the Executive Committee went to Washington, D.C., for the National Welfare Rights convention, and this experience not only gave prestige to the leaders, but also exposed them to what was going on in welfare rights throughout the country.

The four months that the organizers spent in Hinds County assisted the welfare recipients in establishing the Hinds County Welfare Rights Organization. A viable structure was formed with a significant leadership cadre who could function adequately as welfare rights leaders. The welfare movement soon was known throughout the state and sufficient action had been taken against the Hinds County Welfare Department to make it fear and respect a welfare rights organization.

Another important outcome was that the welfare rights movement had gained respectability and prestige in the black community. The fact that the Hinds County WRO assisted Charles Evers in the Poor People's March in Jackson attested to this. The NAACP too often appears to cooperate only with "reputable" organizations. Factors of respect and prestige are important because they secure for the welfare movement necessary aid from other leaders in the black community. They also provided the clients with pride: that essential commodity in reversing the cycle of oppression and worthlessness created by the welfare system. Thus, through the WRO, recipients had an organization that not only met their special income needs, but also gave them a mechanism whereby they could participate in the struggle of black people for freedom and justice.

## Ingredients for Success

As the organizers worked in the county, certain factors were present that aided them in their pursuit of a welfare movement. Some of these, such as the right climate for organizing and large numbers of welfare recipients, were mentioned previously. However, there are other factors that should also be noted.

The repressive nature of the welfare system was an important factor guiding the organizing effort. The conditions for those on welfare were so intolerable that people felt they had little to lose by fighting the welfare department. A small concession, such as being addressed by caseworkers as "Mr." or "Mrs.," was a big victory for the movement because no white in Mississippi used courtesy titles in relationships with black people. The majority of caseworkers, moreover, were unfamiliar with the laws of the system, and when challenged, they often gave in rather than lose face in front of the client. In addition, so many of their practices were so thoroughly racist that the organizers were able to get them removed as they confronted the system. One example comes from Rankin County: the welfare department there refused to grant aid to mothers who had illegitimate children. This was such a flagrant violation of the law that just the threat of a fair hearing ended the policy.

Added to the repression of the system, the mentality of southern welfare workers also worked on behalf of the organizing process. The white southern workers dreaded conflict. A great concern with being liked was responsible for the omnipresent hospitality of the workers; they were (if you will) friendly racists. The paternalistic attitude toward the recipient and the worker's belief that he was truly a helping person made him an easy target for the techniques of organization through confrontation.

When organizers would go into the welfare center and fight for the recipients' rights by screaming, pounding on desks, filing fair hearings and picketing, the pressure became unbearable. To avoid conflict at any price was the goal of the welfare workers, and therefore many concessions were made. With each concession, clients began to see that being organized helped them gain their rights.

Moreover, when the WRO leadership began talking as

equals with department officials, the workers were off guard and fearful. The recipients were beginning to smash the stereotypes that southern whites had about black people. And every confrontation with the welfare workers furthered the clients' realization of the vulnerability of their oppressors. This led to self-confidence and the beginning of a new role image.

## Roadblocks to Progress

With the advantages, there were also certain other factors which hindered welfare organizing. First, the primitive nature of the welfare system made it difficult to meet the needs of the people under any circumstances at all. There were only four categories of aid: Aid to the Blind, Aid to the Disabled, Aid to the Aged, and Aid to Dependent Children. The average ADC check for a *family of four* was $34 a month. Also, in the ADC category, Mississippi paid only 27 per cent of minimum need. There was no medical assistance, emergency assistance, special clothing grants, separate rent money, or furniture grants. If their children were over two years of age, mothers were forced to work—almost 100 per cent of the time in jobs like domestic service at $2 or $3 a day. Thus, even forcing workers to follow the law to the letter, the basic needs of the clients could not be met. Because a plan to fully meet the basic needs of recipients could only be long-range, the organizers focused their action on getting people on the rolls, complicating case closings, obtaining small concessions, and filing fair hearings. These actions would serve to build the movement in the beginning, and, it was hoped, some of the basic needs would gradually be met by constant pressure.

Lack of transportation was an obstacle. There just was not any way for people to get to the welfare center or to meetings except by being driven, and the organizers therefore spent precious time as chauffeurs. If there were to be a meeting or demonstration, workers had to go and pick up most of the people, leaving them dependent on the organizers. This situation remained after the organizers left, with the result that a great number of people who wanted to participate regularly in the WRO could not do so.

Fear also played a role in making organization difficult. The fear of many recipients in the black community was not unrealistic. People had not forgotten the shootings and church burnings of the past. The white community, especially in the rurals, was still hostile and made threats whenever any stirrings occurred in the black community. In the city this also was a problem, but not nearly as severe as in the rural areas of the county.

It was for this reason that workers were cautious and always stayed within the law. Demonstrations and other confrontations were well planned so as to avoid police retaliation. This was done because if the movement elicited police action too quickly it would have fed the fear that was already present and have destroyed the welfare organization.

Weighing both advantages and disadvantages, the summer was successful. A fairly strong welfare rights organization existed. It would need a great deal of support from the CDA staff and the black community, but it had gained a reputation and an executive leadership that would make this support available. The seeds had been planted. The tree was a young one, but it would grow.

## Three Phases of Community Organization

What has preceded is a descriptive survey of the growth of a welfare rights organization in Jackson, Mississippi. However, underlying the visible actions taken is a methodology which may not be apparent to the recipients but which is distinct to the organizer. It involves three phases of growth that a group can be brought through in welfare organizing in Brooklyn, New York, or Jackson, Mississippi. In each of the three phases that exist in welfare organizing, the role of the organizer is distinct and different.

1) The first stage involves a dependency (i.e., the existence of the welfare movement depends on the organizers). Recipients ask what they should do and how they should do it. There is a great fear of taking the initiative, and often the people will not speak freely to challenge the organizer. Knowledge of the law and of their rights is minimal, and recipients stand in awe of the welfare department and the caseworkers. There is also a preoccupation with individual rather than group demands. Every discussion will revolve around each client's personal difficulties. In this phase, the clients will seek to exploit the worker by having him do all the work to get them additional money. They will sit quietly when with the organizer, or use excessive compliments and appeal to his guilt. Sometimes the manipulation is conscious, sometimes unconscious.

In this dependent organizational phase, the organizer functions as an *advocate*. He actively fights for the rights of the recipients. He spends most of his time in the welfare center with the people. He yells, threatens, and constantly harasses the authorities in order to win for the people what is rightfully theirs. At meetings he may do most of the talking. Frequently, if he cannot be present, a meeting will not be held.

In this phase, the organizer, by a conscious use of self, seeks to exploit the weaknesses of the welfare system. He accompanies a client (or preferably a group of clients) to the center, constantly pointing out the inconsistencies, the lies, and the fallibility of the caseworkers. The organizer deliberately uses confrontation as a teaching device. For example, when he sits with the client and his worker, he points out to the recipient where the worker is wrong, when the worker is being too personal or asking questions that are irrelevant, and consciously seeks to make the investigator lose his temper and explode. When he has succeeded, the organizer calmly points out to the client why the worker "lost his cool."

In this phase, the organizer should not become "chummy" with the officials. He should never negotiate without recipients present, even if it will mean that his demands will not be met. The organizer must communicate to the clients that the welfare system is the enemy. No matter how kind the workers seem, they are part of an evil and oppressive system that must be changed.

In this initial phase, the organizer should be careful about being a "hero." To go to jail might not affect the organizer, but it surely will affect the recipients. The organizer should avoid that which is flashy and flamboyant. Often such tactics frighten recipients who are just beginning to throw off the vestiges of oppression. All tactics are a means to building independence on the part of the people. The organizer must constantly strive to have the recipients gradually take the initiative.

2) The second phase is that of quasi-dependent organization. The worker's role is that of an organizer-educator. Having won the confidence of the recipients, the organizer seeks to develop an organizational structure. He stresses group action as opposed to individual action.

It is in this phase that workshops are used at which welfare law is explained. The organizer tries to reduce his role as the center of the movement, and begins a supportive role. He is active, but at the same time he forces the groups to begin making their own decisions. The organizer should allow the group to make their own plans and form their own strategies even though these may be too ambitious or prone to failure. Often a so-called failure, organized and executed by the recipients themselves, is a victory in that they will have learned much and, most importantly, will have exercised their independence.

In this second phase, the people should begin to become group-conscious, more articulate, and self-confident. Leadership begins to emerge. A certain spirit begins to come to the fore. With each confrontation, the recipients gain an identity and pride. They begin to identify with the welfare rights movement.

Following every action should be a critique by the leadership. By learning how to plan, execute, and finally re-evaluate, the recipients' leaders gain insight into the processes of community organization. Slowly they appreciate their actions and become aware of themselves as leaders. They also begin to experience new role models, and when this happens the group is on its way to independence.

3) The third phase should be the establishment of an autonomous organization that is able to plan and carry out actions independent of the organizer. His role in this phase is one of resource person (who is merely consulted by the clients). In this phase there should be sufficient leaders to carry out actions and make daily decisions concerning the organization. When this phase is reached, organizers are used primarily for research and training of new members. In many cities across the country, Welfare Rights Organizations are in this stage.

## Experience: North and South

Based on the experiences of organizers who have worked both in New York and Mississippi, these three phases exist in organizing in both areas. The difference lies in the speed with which an organizer can move from Phase I to Phases II and III. Due to the repressive nature of the welfare system and the life-style of the black population in Mississippi, the process is much slower. The political climate and white intransigence in racial situations forces the organizer in Mississippi to be more cautious in planning each phase with the group. He must avoid confrontations which will elicit repressive action (jailing, shooting, economic intimidation) from the establishment. This framework differs greatly from that in New York where radical action (sit-ins occasionally for days at a time, harassment of workers, center take-overs) generally can be initiated without fear of physical harm.

In New York there are many dedicated professionals (social workers, lawyers, politicians) and civic groups who have aligned themselves with the Welfare Rights Organization and act to support WRO actions in bringing pressure on the system, preventing it from taking severe retaliatory actions. In Mississippi, such outside support is critically deficient, and the Welfare Rights Movement mainly operates on its own two feet, absorbing all costs.

The character of the welfare system in Mississippi is that of a close-knit family. Each county office knows what its brothers are doing, and an attack on one is an attack on all that becomes known quickly throughout the state. In New York, the character of the welfare system is that of a business. Each neighborhood office acts autonomously to the extent that the bureaucratic maze keeps offices separated from each other and from the city's headquarters.

These factors—with their corresponding organizing limitations—constitute the differences in welfare rights organizing North and South. The three phases are always operable, but within each phase, action must be modified to meet the specifications of the people and the locale. The Mississippi welfare client will take longer to be organized, but he can ultimately become a militant leader along with his counterpart from the North.

## STUDY QUESTIONS

1. Do you agree with the worker's assessment that welfare rights was the appropriate organizing vehicle for the county under the stated conditions? Why? What might have been some options?

2. What does the writer mean when he says that welfare recipients are treated as "nonpersons"? Can you give other examples from your practice experience of nonpersons in our social system?

3. In his description of the worker's approach to the community ("The Early Experience"), the author outlines a pattern of intervention that begins with meetings with the county leaders and proceeds to small meetings with welfare

recipients in homes and churches. Does this approach seem to you to be an advisable one? Would you make any changes if you were the worker?

4. Arundell emphasizes that the workers must create a polarization in which the welfare department is clearly perceived as the enemy. What are the advantages (and disadvantages) of such a strategy? Is there an alternative strategy that you would prefer?

5. "And with each new [welfare department] concession, a new demand was made." Why is this approach suggested?

6. Many of the black leaders of the community were critical of the mass rally and march of June 30th. On what grounds do you think it is open to criticism as being organizationally dysfunctional?

7. Arundell implies that the organizers were remarkably successful in establishing the beginning of a welfare rights organization in the county in the four months of the summer. Does this seem realistic in terms of your experience in working with groups and organizations?

8. The author suggests that there are secondary benefits to welfare rights organizing. For example, he stresses that it instills pride, is a vehicle for group participation, and may favorably affect one's self-image. How important do you feel these other outcomes are in relation to the goals of the welfare rights movement?

9. The author suggests that there were flagrant violations of the law in the administration of public welfare (citing the refusal to grant ADC to mothers with illegitimate children as an example). How could these flagrant violations have persisted in a program that is under the supervision of both the state and federal governments? What are the implications for social welfare administration?

10. It is suggested that the local welfare workers were paternalistic with clients, dreaded confrontation, and avoided conflict at all costs. Do you feel such reactions are particularly southern, or are they characteristic of workers in similar circumstances North and South? Explain.

11. Are the welfare agents really the "oppressors" in the system? If so, why? If not, why not—and who are?

12. Discuss the role of client fear in community organization. What can the organizer do to mitigate fear, and yet remain within the bounds of realism so as not to jeopardize the safety of his clients and their organization?

13. Arundell suggests that in the first phase of organizing there is a preoccupation with individual rather than group demands. Do you agree? Is this justified in terms of the long-range goals and the need for early organizational activity?

14. The worker "should never negotiate without recipients present, even if it will mean that his demands will not be met." Do you agree or disagree with this statement? Why?

15. In Phase II, Arundell suggests that "the organizer should allow the group to make their own plans and form their own strategies even though these may be too ambitious or prone to failure." Discuss the merits of this proposition.

16. In his three phases of organizing, Arundell sees the worker successively as advocate, educator and consultant. Do you agree with these roles for the worker? How are these roles similar to (and how in turn do they differ from) those suggested by Kurzman and Solomon in the opening articles of this book?

17. In comparing the welfare system, North and South, the author suggests that the Mississippi system resembles a close-knit family, while the New York counterpart is more like a business. Would you agree with his conclusion? What would be the implications of such a situation for welfare rights organizing, North and South?

# Paraprofessionals in the North and South: A Black Critique

GARDENIA WHITE

## The Paraprofessional Role

Servicing the poor has created a new job category: the paraprofessional. The reluctance of many professionals to work with the poor has limited the supply of trained personnel. Consequently, there is a great need for supporting aides from the indigenous community. Also, these new paraprofessional jobs provide opportunities for a large number of poor people, thus helping to reduce poverty by turning people on welfare into reading assistants, delinquents into researchers, and students into tutors.

The role of the indigenous staffs is to serve as "bridge" people: interpreting community life and values to professionals, on the one hand; and interpreting the professional to the community, on the other hand. In helping bridge the gap, paraprofessionals make services available and less impersonal to the community. They also free professionals to perform

Adapted with permission of the Institute of Community Studies, Queens College, from *Community*, Vol. 1, No. 2 (January, 1969).

more technical tasks and to work under considerably less pressure.

Moreover, paraprofessionals often function as models to other community residents. Therefore, paraprofessionals can become decisive factors in helping treatment agencies reorganize their approaches to low-income people.

However, there are difficulties in the paraprofessional-professional relationship. My experience as a black paraprofessional, both in the North and South, bears that out. But the experiences were different.

## The Southern Experience

In the summer of 1967, I was one of several people volunteering their services in Mississippi to work with the Community Development Agency of the Michael Schwerner Memorial Fund. The other people included three white and one black professional. I worked with the black professional, a social work student from the Columbia University School of Social Work.

We helped in a variety of ways. We assisted people in applying for aid; took them to city hospitals; and obtained food and clothing from the Salvation Army. In short, we helped at whatever was needed.

As a black worker in a Mississippi community, I was admired for being able to stand up to white people and for caring about the community. I was one of "them," understanding "the problem" because I myself had lived with the problem. A mother would feel more comfortable telling me about the welfare department, how her children couldn't go to school because they didn't have any shoes, about the health services she could not get for her children because she had no money. Telling this to a white person is difficult because there is a tendency not to be honest and straightforward. Black southerners view all white people as professionals.

One of the ways I was able to help was by sitting with clients in the Department of Welfare. For example, the first thing the local worker would do to demoralize both of us would be to say in a very patronizing way, "What do you want?" I would then very calmly introduce the client as Mrs. X from Pocahontas, and "I am Mrs. White from The Hinds County Welfare Rights Movement." The social worker would then address me as Mrs. White, but would continue to address the client as Mary (or never mentioning her name at all). Just by having the worker address me, a black person, as "Mrs." made a difference to the client.

The black community in Mississippi viewed the social work student and me as black people helping them. There was no professional-nonprofessional distinction. I would mention from time to time to the clients that she was a professional and I was just a community worker, but they never paid any attention to this. To them, I was just as professional as she was; I had a certain set of skills that could be used to help them, and that was all that mattered.

## The Northern Experience

My experience in the North has been different. I am a New Yorker, and I have been actively involved in the community. Most of my work here has been with white professionals.

I have lived in the community where I am now for twelve years; my children have gone to the community schools. I have always been extremely community-conscious, especially concerning the schools, and am determined that my children receive a good education. It is also clear to me that it is not enough that only *my* children be educated. All minority children deserve a good education.

When the poverty program was established a few years ago in my neighborhood, I got a job as an aide in a parent education program. I worked primarily with black parents, visiting them in their homes. I set up workshops for parents on topics like sex education, helped parents interpret report cards and obtain their children's reading scores, and sat with them at school suspension hearings. The aim of these activities, of course, was to get parents to take a more active role in the education of their children.

In the North, I found a major problem between professionals and nonprofessionals. Complaints by paraprofessionals are made that professionals have nicer offices, are treated better, have secretaries, are recognized by other professionals, etc. Complaints are made by paraprofessionals that professionals show favoritism within the nonprofessional staff.

These grievances are an important factor because they often work against a cooperative relationship between the nonprofessional and the professional, and this relation is often contaminated by the professional's lack of respect for the nonprofessional. In other words, there are some condescending attitudes of professionals toward nonprofessionals. These are legitimate causes for strain, but are compounded by hostile attitudes among nonprofessionals that often are irrational, self-defeating and destructive to the harmonious functioning of a team.

Many paraprofessionals who have more education and a middle-class background are substituted for indigenous low-income personnel. Some professionals find it easier to work with the better-educated nonprofessionals who are more like themselves. Unfortunately, these middle-class nonprofessionals do not possess the relationship to the low-income community necessary for effective interclass communication. Therefore, in the long run, what seems easier may produce new difficulties. One of them is that the whole operation becomes distorted in order to fit the skills and limitations of the middle-class professional.

Also, there is the tendency on the part of some indigenous nonprofessionals to feel superior toward their less fortunate peers among the poor. Some of them acquire many of the prevailing middle-class attitudes toward the poor: that persons are responsible for their social circumstances; that those who do not pay for a service are getting a "favor." These attitudes may stem partly from a negative self-image and internalization of middle-class viewpoints; they could also be a reaction of persons who have bettered themselves, even if slightly, in relation to the group from which they have come.

Professional workers also harbor prejudice toward clients, but tend to express it in subtler ways that are, nonetheless, very apparent to low-income clients. Professionals having this attitude should be clearly exposed and opposed.

## STUDY QUESTIONS

1. The writer indicates that black mothers in Mississippi felt more comfortable speaking with her, as another black person, than they did with whites. Do you think this phenomenon would be equally true in the North?

2. Why did the Mississippi welfare worker address the author (a black paraprofessional) with last name and courtesy title—when she would address the client (also a black woman and about the same age) by first name only?

3. The writer suggests that the black Mississippi clients did not differentiate between black professionals and paraprofessionals. Would this be true in a similar situation in the North?

4. Do you feel that the major problems suggested between professionals and paraprofessionals in the North are more a function of role and status, or of race? Explain your answer.

5. It is suggested that paraprofessionals are often selected by professionals more on the basis of their capacity for communicating with their middle-class supervisors than for their ability to function among lower-class clients. Based on your practice experience, do you agree or disagree with this observation? What are some of the dangers inherent in the selection of paraprofessionals by a nonresident, middle-class, professional supervisory staff?

6. How can one seek to mitigate the tendency on the part of some indigenous paraprofessionals to internalize middle-class values and thereby separate themselves from the people

they serve? Is this necessarily a great danger? Are there ways in which internalization of some professional and middle-class values can become functional to the paraprofessional worker?

# The Worker as Transient:
# A Practice Model

BARBARA A. SCHRAM

There is a growing interest in the time dimension in the social work process. Starting with the Rankians, and extending to current experiments with provocative therapy and encounter groups, there is an increasing interest in speeding up the therapeutic process. The interest has grown not only out of a professional commitment to sharpen skills, but also out of the very pragmatic considerations of limited-period grant programs and demonstration projects. The advent of the federal poverty program has forced social work practitioners to demonstrate to their clients (as well as to the public at large) how much they can help people accomplish in defined periods of time.

Within the field of community organization the development of speeded-up, time-phased programs has been particularly evident. The vagaries of funds as well as the growing tensions in our country have mandated the urgent development of interventions and training skills that accomplish dramatic organizational results. Funding as well as political problems have made the tenure of community programs so unsure that the worker cannot count on long periods in which to build relationships with clients and community groups. Programs are cut back without warning, with little consideration as to the phase the operation happens to be in.

And even where the government may be willing, long-pent-up angers of the black poor have been manifested in justifiable impatience. They have little confidence in traditional, slow-moving channels for social change and often view the professional social worker, *especially* the white one, as an impediment—ineffective and damaging. If he is to be useful, therefore, the professional must prove he has a set of skills that can help people obtain changes of a real nature in a short period of time. He must also be aware that the gains the group makes will be doubly greater if they achieve them with their *own* leadership. The worker therefore must develop the ability not only to act quickly and effectively himself, but to transfer his skills to the group members themselves.

In the training of community organizers the pressures of time and the effective transfer of skills to local leadership have not always been prime concerns. Now, however, we must begin to develop models of practice to meet such recently articulated needs in the field.

## The Mississippi Setting

The opportunity to come to grips with the development of "transient organizers" is afforded by a project such as the Michael Schwerner Memorial Fund has sponsored year-round in Hinds County, Mississippi. Each summer, professional social workers have come to work in the Welfare Rights Movement arm of the program there for periods as short as three weeks. The worker who arrives for a three-week stay never loses his awareness that the days of beginning and ending his work are telescoped into a small moment of life. The injustice he confronts is of such an order of gravity and the needs of people are of such immediate concern that he must begin to function virtually the moment he steps off the airplane. The worker in this type of situation must begin his tasks without any of the usual orientation period that has marked his work in more traditional settings in the past. He may expect to find that his clients are ready to receive his help without the usual period of relationship building. They are desperately in need of help and the agency he will represent is the only one in the county that is set up to give service to poor black people free from the punitive and degrading atmosphere that so often characterizes the traditional southern social work establishment. The new worker is generally seen as the extension of the one who has preceded him, and, in fact, the original introduction to the client is usually made on this basis. The new worker says, "Ronald told me you wanted someone to go to the welfare office with you"—and the client is ready to relate. Given the receptivity of the clients and the constantly emerging work tasks, let us look at some of the usual areas of worker activity and see how they are carried out in the telescoped experience.

### Setting the Contract

Before entering into a working relationship, traditional practice dictates that we must clearly define what services we are prepared to offer and how we will go about offering them. We generally work to establish the contract between ourself and our clients through a series of varied interactions. As the relationship between client and worker progresses, the contract is made progressively clearer through a process of testing act against response. In the "instant relationship" we must achieve in our role as a transient professional, we cannot count on a series of varied interactions with either our clients or the welfare workers. We must, in the first (and perhaps only) encounter make the contract explicitly clear. Our working contract in Mississippi, for example, defined us as the *employee* of the clients, there for a limited time to help them learn how to achieve their rights in dealing with the welfare system. We must find ways to demonstrate the contract immediately in the most dramatic fashion possible. We cannot risk having either client or welfare worker unsure of our stance or commitment.

For example, when accompanying clients into a welfare interview we can support our verbal statement that we are their employee by sitting at their side and relating only to them, refusing to enter into any private relationship with the white welfare worker. By breaking into the interview between client and welfare agent and openly questioning the validity of the agent's statements or questions, we also show our function. When we drive clients to and from interviews, serve them coffee, and call them Mr. and Mrs., we are showing our clients in no uncertain terms that we regard them as people of worth and we are prepared to do what *they* define as needed tasks.

## Examples from Practice

Although we are flying in the face of traditional, predictable relationships by the way we define our contract, in practice it seems to be understood. While we were speaking with people in the waiting room of the Hinds County Welfare Department, a woman whom we did not know approached us and told us that the welfare agents were trying to take a small child away from a neighbor who was sheltering her until her absent mother returned. She asked us to go to the neighbor and help her figure out the legal rights of the mother. She seemed to be fairly certain that we would not report the whereabouts of the child to the welfare department and that we would champion the cause of the absent mother. As we searched the neighborhood for the child, the woman told people at each home that we were "all right" and that they could tell us what they knew.

Similarly, in any dealings we have with welfare workers we must immediately demonstrate the contract under which we operate. The welfare workers, assuming we are somehow "one of them" because we are white, often attempt to implicate us in their typical patterns of relationships. In one rural county welfare office a young social worker invited the northern worker to come into her office for a "professional" talk. The worker accepted the invitation, but brought along with her the local leaders of the welfare rights group, explaining that anything that she as a worker had to say would be of interest to welfare clients. During the interview the worker withdrew from the conversation, busying herself taking notes, while the local leaders used the opportunity to present their demands to the welfare worker who had previously refused to meet with them.

The worker, then, spends little time on verbal delineation of contract. Instead, he finds opportunities to *demonstrate* the contract dramatically—preferably within the first few moments of any encounter with a client or welfare agent.

As the encounter ends, the worker completes the contract by explaining that while *he* may not be present at the next meeting or interview, another worker, operating in the same manner, will replace him.

## Assessment and Diagnosis

In the traditional setting, the worker would begin his assessment of the needs of a group by speaking with its members, reading records, and consulting with other professionals who are aware of its performance. Given the sketchy nature of recordings left by past workers in a civil rights project, the great difficulty of visiting homes scattered over the county before a meeting is held, and the worker turnover implicit in the concept of transiency, the diagnosis of the worker must generally be made within the opening minutes of the meeting itself. He asks the clients to tell him briefly what they have been working on and what they had planned to do at this meeting. If they have no plan or project in mind, he must provoke a discussion so he can determine which items seem to evoke the most response. The cohesion of the group, its readiness to act, and its leadership patterns must be assessed from moment to moment. Additionally, the worker must assess what use the group can make of him, and in what way his presence may be masking or deflecting the real items they wish to work on.

The same philosophy of immersion must characterize individual relationships. In Mississippi, workers often went right into welfare department waiting rooms and offered to help clients negotiate their upcoming interviews with the welfare agents. The worker in this setting rarely had time for more than a ten-minute conversation preparatory to the interview. The worker had to develop a set of sharply clear questions so that he could determine how the facts would fit the welfare requirement and how the client would hold up in the upcoming interview. Whatever the assessment, the worker then must tell the client how he thinks his case stacks up against the regulations and what elements might need to be changed to get his case accepted.

In addition, the worker must decide how much potential for leadership the applicant has, because his primary task as a transient organizer is to build organizations and transfer skill to local people. These—rather than giving help to individual welfare clients—are his *priority* responsibilities. On the basis of his estimates, the worker then offers his services to accompany a few from among the many clients in the waiting room.

The original assessment of the client (and his case) should continue to be modified during the actual encounter with the welfare agent. If the initial assessment needs to be changed drastically, then probably the worker had not focused his initial interview clearly enough, or had not read initial clues properly.

## Worker Intervention

With the contract established and the assessment and diagnosis completed, the transient worker plans and executes his intervention. Needless to say, he is at best on shaky ground. His actions, constructed on the most limited knowledge, will obviously have a large margin of error. He must be able to risk acting, even though very unsure. As he proceeds he must be able to be unabashed by his own errors in judgment and knowledge of a situation, concentrating on developing skills in *recouping and capitalizing on these errors*. It often happens, for example, that the worker challenges a welfare agent on a point of state welfare law with which he is unfamiliar. He demands to see written proof, and even if the agent proves to be correct, he then points out to the client that agents often distort and are never to be trusted. In a similar manner, a new volunteer worker was confused about the day the Schwerner Fund was to accompany clients to the welfare department, and arrived on the wrong day. When challenged by the welfare agent, the volunteer announced that he wanted to see how people were treated when the volunteers were *not* around. It did turn out, in fact, that people were being severely abused that day just as they had been before the Welfare Rights Movement began. The workers then took turns "dropping in" to the welfare office on unexpected days to attempt to force the agency to maintain a higher standard of client treatment (even though the volunteers did *not* have the manpower to service the center on a daily basis).

Hence, the worker can use his errors as well as his successes as training devices for clients. By making explicit everything the actors in the situation are doing, the worker and client can evaluate an interaction after it is over. Through this process of consciously looking at acts, the worker helps clients sharpen their own negotiation and intervention skills. Similarly, after a training meeting, the worker must point out why he did certain things, e.g., "I used the role play because I think acting things out in front of the group helps a lot to prepare people. I think they find it a little easier to talk back to the white welfare agent after the way they talked back to me."

## Recording

The need for recording (to pass on to the next worker as well as to indigenous welfare leaders) is an obvious one. The need, however, is often neglected as workers yield to pressures to be out in the field doing rather than dictating in an office. The worker, therefore, must develop a recording format to state in simple, brief language what happened, with whom, what follow-ups are planned or indicated, and what his recommendations would be for the next transient worker in subsequent encounters. The format the doctor uses for notations on the back of a patient's card is perhaps the closest parallel type of recording we can suggest. Notes must be brief and immediately useful to either professional or indigenous organizers. Here, as in all other worker activities, the products are the property of the group and should be useful to *them* in increasing *their* skill to carry on.

The worker should also attempt to sum up the knowledge he has gained during his tenure. A body of these insights can form the basis of simple printed training materials that transmit through words and pictures some of the essential ingredients: welfare laws, meeting formats that worked well, and any deals that have been negotiated during his tenure.

## Miscellaneous Chores

The social worker must recognize and accept the fact that when he arrives in an organization it may not at that stage in its evolution need the skills he is most competent to offer. He may find, for example, that the people are preparing a large demonstration and that, rather than giving training sessions, his skills as carpenter or sign painter are more immediately valuable. Again, he may find that transporting group members to and from meetings is his most valuable contribution. On the other hand, he may find that his ability to understand poverty program guidelines is his most useful asset and he may find himself stuck in an office, writing a proposal for his entire stay with the organization. If he fully accepts his "employee" function, then the needs of the members determine his activities. This is what transient organizing is all about.

## Assets and Liabilities in the Use of Transient Workers

Thus far, we have explored some of the basic worker tasks and seen how they are adapted to fit the conditions of limited-time organizing. Now we will explore the implications of transient practice.

### 1. Assets

a. *Genuine clarity of worker-client relationship can be achieved.*

The short tenure of the worker, propelling him to give and get information quickly, tends to cut down the credibility gap so often present in traditional, long-term worker-client relationships. Neither client nor worker can afford to spend time inferring what the other may mean by a particular behavior. If they actually engage in establishing a clear contract and are making their activities explicit, then their relationship must be marked by a high degree of honesty and frankness.

In addition, the removal of the traditional aspects of the "social agency" (desks, secretaries, appointments, working hours, etc.) brings both worker and client closer together. To a far greater degree than in a traditional setting, they become two people jointly engaged in a common task. The success or failure of the worker in a particular encounter is a topic of open discussion between himself and the clients. The process of *direct accountability* of worker to client is strengthened in this atmosphere. Finally, the constant change in workers helps avoid the trap of dependency in the worker-client relationship. Neither party can afford to become too emotionally involved nor can either one try to hold on to the other . . . the letting-go process is within the *nature* of the situation.

b. *Wide variety of worker style and expertise is made available to the group.*

The group has available for its use a far greater range of expertise than it could ever be afforded by one or two full-time workers. The variations among worker styles can be drawn upon. Additionally, clients may be able to find, in the variety, intervention styles and techniques best adapted to their own personality and style.

c. *The movement gains the "illusion of power" before it may in fact have it.*

The constantly changing faces and styles of workers make it difficult for the white power structure to accurately gauge the amount of consultative strength a group has at its disposal. On the outside, it often looks as if the group has an enormous and highly specialized professional staff. Outsiders have no way of knowing what the tenure of individual workers may be. And, in the eyes of the black community, the constant influx of outside professionals gives the group some status, and an aura of solidity and security.

## 2. Liabilities

a. *There can be a lack of adequate follow-up in transition periods.*

When a new worker takes over from a departing colleague, he assumes all the obligations and commitments that the former worker has made. Through insufficient recording or overambitious commitments, the transient worker may have left assignments that cannot realistically be fulfilled. A client can be kept waiting for a worker who never comes or a group may have planned a major meeting that must go unstaffed. Obviously, this cutting off of help already started or promised can drive the poor person deeper into feelings of hopelessness and despair. It can also engender a suspicion and bitterness toward organizing that will take a long time to repair.

b. *Breaks in continuity between workers.*

Too long a break in time between the tenure of workers can often slow down the growth of an organization. Groups may keep repeating activities they have learned instead of initiating the new projects that keep members committed and help organizations to grow.

In addition, the white establishment which has been forced to deal with the organization may perceive that it has only to sit out the tenure of the worker. Then it will renege on arrangements made, perhaps retaliating against the clients in the process. If the movement is not yet strong enough to stand on its own base of power, the members may suffer more from the lack of staff continuity than they were suffering before the group itself ever started.

c. *Disconnections may occur between consecutive worker styles.*

Until an organization has a strong life of its own, the worker and his methods have a strong influence on it. If, because of poor orientation and selection procedures, the styles of succeeding workers are drastically different, the group may experience a kind of programmatic schizophrenia. One month, its members may plan a strategy only to have it diverted the next month by a worker who thinks it a dangerous or ineffective one. In addition to causing enormous confusion among members, very different worker approaches may tend to generate factions and cliques which support the varying styles. The white community, sensitive to any breaks in group cohesion, can then drive the wedge further into the group by playing off one faction against another, or by sitting out a negotiation, hoping that the worker will turn its course to their advantage.

## *Summary*

We have attempted to delineate the skills needed by a professional community organizer in a transient, time-limited assignment. We have used the experiences gained from welfare rights organizing in the South as a case in point. We looked at the tasks of contract setting, assessment and evaluation, and intervention and recording—and we have seen that in each, common elements persist. The basic component is direct honesty and openness in the worker-client relationship, where it is made demonstrably clear that the worker is an employee of the client. In this context the worker becomes an advocate for the client at the same time as he is a teacher of advocacy skills.

We have suggested that the time-limited situation is one of high risk with a large potential for error. We feel this to be mitigated, however, by constant evaluation and discussion between client and worker, which can turn every encounter into a learning situation. Moreover, we see the opportunity of direct accountability of worker to client as a major asset of the transient situation.

We feel that the use of time-limited community organizers is a growing reality in the field and that it offers opportunities to build indigenous organizations and thereby speed up the process of social change.

STUDY QUESTIONS

1. The author states that "in the training of community organizers, the pressures of time and the effective transfer of skills to local leadership have not always been prime concerns." Do you agree or disagree with this statement?

2. What is meant by the expression "setting the contract" between client and worker? How important is such a process in social work practice?

3. What do you think of a contract that defines the worker essentially as the employee of the client? Is such a contract appropriate to social work?

4. The author feels it is important to demonstrate the above contract to the adversary (i.e., welfare agents) early in the working relationship. Do you agree or disagree? Why?

5. Is it realistic to expect a transient worker to make a community assessment under the conditions imposed by the setting and his short-term status? What are some of the advantages of making such an early assessment? What are some of the pitfalls?

6. In social work, traditionally we have stressed the important roles of client-worker understanding and relationship building. Is the diminished emphasis on relationship in the helping process here advisable in terms of what you know about social work practice?

7. Is it proper professional practice for the organizer to deliberately encourage client distrust of the workers in a social welfare system? Discuss.

8. The writer has placed a stress upon the importance of recording—but not in order to evaluate or review the worker's performance so much as to provide an ongoing log of information to serve the client group. What do you feel are the merits (and demerits) of such an approach to case recording?

9. Reference is made to a "credibility gap" in traditional client-worker relationships. To what do you believe the writer could be referring? Do you agree with her? Explain.

10. Schram here suggests that there are advantages in a process of direct accountability of worker to client—over the indirect (supervisor and/or agency-monitored) process to which social workers are generally accustomed. What is your reaction?

11. What is meant by the organization's need for developing "the illusion of power"? Do you think it is a helpful concept? An appropriate one for social work practice?

12. Do you feel workers can provide sufficient continuity

in process and relationships to make a model of transiency effective? Have you ever seen such a model in practice in other settings without specifically being defined as such? What are the implications?

13. In reviewing the list of "assets" and "liabilities" of transiency provided by the author, can you provide further examples? In weighing the assets and liabilities, what is your opinion regarding the potential effectiveness of the transient worker model?

*PART III*

# CASE STUDIES

# The Porter Family Social Study

JUDITH BEYMAN

This is a brief social history of the Porter family, a black family residing in Jackson, Mississippi.

Mrs. Edna Lee Wilson Porter was born in Yazoo City, Mississippi, on August 12, 1920. Her parents were not married when she was born; they married soon after her birth. Her mother, Hattie Bell White, and her father, Ed Wilson, were sharecroppers. Five children were born of this union. Mrs. Porter's parents soon separated and her mother had three common-law husbands in succession.

Mrs. Porter's parents were mobile. Their frequent moves from one sharecropper farm to another were made in an attempt to find a good "boss man." Characteristic of most sharecroppers, Mrs. Porter's family borrowed money to live and had to pick and chop cotton to "work off" their loan. Becoming frustrated with the futility of paying off such impossible debts, and trying to better themselves, they usually escaped in the dark of night without paying.

Adapted with permission of the Association of Black Social Workers from *Black Caucus,* Vol. 1, No. 1 (Fall, 1968), pp. 49–58. The account is factual, but the names have been changed to protect the parties involved, as is true in other similar references throughout this book.

FACE SHEET DATA

Mrs. Edna Lee Wilson Porter—Mother
218 Market Street
Jackson, Mississippi
b/d August 12, 1920
b/p Yazoo City, Mississippi

*Porter Children and Grandchildren*
1)  Carrie Porter                     Edna Lee Wilson Porter—mother
    b/d Sept. 18, 1944                       Frank Porter—father
    b/p Inverness, Miss. (by midwife)
    Carrie is blind and mentally retarded.

        *Carrie's offspring*
        a)  Jesse Jr. Porter*—father, Jesse Barnes
            b/d July 20, 1962
            b/p Greenwood, Miss. (Greenwood Le
                Flora Hospital)
        b)  Karl Lee Porter*—father, Jesse Barnes
            b/d Aug. 10, 1963
            b/p Jackson, Miss. (University Hospital)
            Karl was born prematurely and is mentally
                retarded.

2)  Frances Lee Porter Gray*      Edna Lee Wilson Porter—mother
    b/d Oct. 18, 1946                       Frank Porter—father
    b/p Belzonia, Miss. (midwife)

        *Frances' offspring*
        a)  Helen Porter*—father, T. D. Smith
            b/d Oct. 28, 1962
            b/p Jackson, Miss. (midwife)
            Helen has had polio, whooping cough,
                frequent colds and impetigo.

* These children reside with Mrs. Porter.

3) Mary Lee Porter Green   Edna Lee Wilson Porter—mother
 b/d Dec. 17, 1947      Frank Porter—father
 b/p Belzonia, Miss.

   *Mary's offspring*
   a) James Allan Green
    b/d July 20, 1965
    b/p Jackson, Miss. (University Hospital)
   b) Senta Green
    b/d Dec. 3, 1966
    b/p Jackson, Miss. (University Hospital)
    Senta died in a fire.

4) Idela Porter        Edna Lee Porter—mother
 b/d July 9, 1949       Frank Porter—father
 b/p Invernness, Miss.

   *Idela's offspring*
   a) Lindsey Lee Porter*—father unknown
    b/d March 12, 1966
    b/p Jackson, Miss. (University Hospital)
   b) Victoria Porter*—father, Walter
     Washington
    b/d April 28, 1967
    b/p Jackson, Miss. (University Hospital)
    Victoria suffers from frequent high fevers
     and vomiting.

5) Frank Porter, Jr.*     Edna Lee Porter—mother
 b/d July 1, 1952      Frank Porter—father
 b/p Sarahal, Miss. (midwife)
6) Robert Lee Porter*    Edna Lee Porter—mother
 b/d Nov. 20, 1954     Frank Porter—father
 b/p Indianola, Miss. (midwife)
7) Frankie Mae Jones*    Edna Lee Porter—mother
 b/d Sept. 8, 1956     Frank Porter—father
 b/p Belzonia, Miss. (midwife)

 * These children reside with Mrs. Porter.

## *The Early Years*

Mrs. Porter recalls being brought up on milk and corn bread and wearing clothing made from flour grain bags. She did not go to school until she was twelve years old. Her family couldn't affort to send her to school and they usually lived too far away. After completing one year of school, Mrs. Porter married Ernest Thomas at the age of thirteen. No children were born of this union and the couple soon separated.

Mrs. Porter and her mother then moved to Le Flora County. There they were sharecroppers and day workers.

She married Frank Porter in the early 1940's. Her life with Frank was one of great hardship. According to her, he was a "very mean man." He often beat her and the children. He was sexually promiscuous and had contracted syphilis. Mrs. Porter remembers eleven pregnancies. Seven children are living, one of whom is mentally retarded and blind. Of the remaining pregnancies, three resulted in miscarriages and one a stillbirth.

When her husband Frank tried to kill her for the second time and beat their daughter, Idela, Mrs. Porter left him (1957). She took the children to live with their relatives in Greenwood, Mississippi. At this time, she applied for welfare but was rejected. She and her older children supported the family by picking cotton for a few dollars a day.

In 1961, Mrs. Porter had a hysterectomy because she had cancer of the womb. Her white boss lady sent Mrs. P. to her own doctor and she was accepted as a charity patient in Greenwood's Le Flora Hospital. Since she was unable to pick cotton after undergoing surgery, she began to receive welfare assistance. She complained that the welfare agent told her how to run her life. She was instructed to use less heat, her relatives were ordered out of the home when the welfare agent visited, and so forth. Although she was still quite ill, she was cut off welfare because the agent said she had a boyfriend. Mrs. Porter denied this, and it was never proved.

Mrs. Porter's landlord, "a good white man," tried to help her get back on welfare. But to the southern racist mind, this only meant that this white man was doing favors for Mrs. Porter because she was his girlfriend. As a result, the welfare department still refused to give aid to the Porter family. In a last attempt to get assistance from the welfare department, Mrs. Porter and the landlord went to the county welfare department. They were told by three white "tough men" that they were not giving her another cent and they forced her to leave the office.

## The Move to Jackson

In 1963, Mrs. Porter finally had to leave Greenwood because her life had been threatened for participating in civil rights activity—this activity merely involved the distribution of NAACP leaflets urging people to stand up for their rights. Mrs. Porter had been picked up by the local police and jailed. Later that night, two men dressed in civilian clothes led her from jail to their car. They rode her around town while hurling abuses and threats at her. Frightened of approaching death, she threw herself from the car. She ran to a crowd but she was helpless as the men tore her clothes away, beat her and led her back to the car. Mrs. Porter was taken back to jail and for hours the police refused to admit to her relatives that she was in jail. She was finally bailed out by civil rights lawyers.

The next day, Mrs. Porter's life was threatened by these men and the police. After consulting with Charles Evers, she decided to escape to Jackson. Her daughter, Frances, was sent to Jackson to find the apartment and the following week the Porter family moved to the big city. It was quite difficult for people who had been sharecroppers and field workers all of their life to earn a living in Jackson. So, for the first few months, Charles Evers paid the family's rent.

When I asked Mrs. Porter about the reason for her concern and involvement in the civil rights movement, she said that she decided to become actively involved after witnessing a police dog gnaw a colored reverend's leg. He had been participating in a civil rights demonstration.

Mrs. Porter has had relatively little trouble in Jackson with the police with the exception of one incident three months ago when she was falsely accused of possessing a gun. Although some witnesses supported her innocence, she was beaten and jailed by a Negro policeman. (Most black people feel that Negro policemen are brutal because of orders received from "peckerwood"—white cops.) With the help of the Lawyer's Committee in Jackson, Mrs. Porter filed suit against the police but she has not heard anything concerning its progress.

About the only good thing that has happened to Mrs. Porter in Jackson is her participation in the STAR antipoverty program. She was paid to take several courses in basic reading and writing from 4:30 to 10:30 every evening for six months. Mrs. Porter said she was "crazy" about it. "Now, I can write a letter." She wants to continue with this program even though she knows that she would not receive any money.

In 1962, Mrs. Porter lived common-law with Jesse Barnes —a "good man," she thought, until she wondered about her oldest daughter's pregnancy. Carrie's emotional retardation had become progressively worse and her sight had declined to the point where she became totally blind at twelve. Carrie gave birth to a child in 1962, and to a mentally retarded child in 1963. Mrs. Porter was suspicious of Barnes but it was several years before he admitted to raping Carrie. Mrs. Porter told me that she was really "hurtin'" when Barnes revealed this. After the second child, the welfare department suggested that Carrie be sterilized. The operation was performed in University Hospital free of charge. At times like these, there seems to exist a relationship between the welfare department and University Hospital to make arrangements for free medical care. (The welfare department has continually denied that they can obtain medical care free of charge for welfare patients.)

## The Children

Two of the Porter girls have had run-ins with racist justice. In 1963, when Idela was fifteen, she ran away from home. Since Idela had been missing for days, Mrs. Porter contacted the Jackson police. She finally found Idela and had her and the boy she had run away with placed in jail to teach them a lesson. The following day, Mr. Cameron, the juvenile officer, visited Mrs. Porter. Having asked Idela about her family's history, Mr. Cameron found out that Mrs. Porter had remarried without obtaining a divorce. He cursed her and threatened her with five years in jail. He told her that he wanted her to put Idela in Whitfield, the local mental hospital. Mrs. Porter refused and demanded that her daughter be released from jail. Mrs. Porter's wishes weren't considered and the next day Cameron placed Idela in Whitfield. (Mrs. Porter states that she never signed any papers to commit her daughter to Whitfield. She also charges Cameron with raping Idela before taking her to Whitfield.) Later that night, Cameron visited Mrs. Porter's house to question her daughter, Mary, about "how many men she had." He took Mary in the kitchen and tried to molest her. Two days later, he tried to force Mrs. Porter to sign papers to put the whole family in Whitfield. Despite her refusal, Cameron was very persistent. Finally, Mrs. Porter grabbed a butcher knife and forced him out of her home. She then told Charles Evers about the situation and he spoke with Cameron; Cameron did not re-enter her home.

In 1965, the black people of Jackson marched through the streets to gain the right to demonstrate. As they walked a few blocks, the police would sweep down and jail these people. The next day another group of marchers would begin to walk, only to be jailed again. Mrs. Porter's daughter,

Frances, participated in these demonstrations. Along with the other marchers, Frances was arrested and taken to the State Fair Grounds. While they were in the Fair Grounds, one of the female marchers cursed a peckerwood officer. Thinking Frances was responsible for this remark, a white officer beat her and placed her in the county jail. The beating was so severe that Frances passed out in jail. She was finally taken to University Hospital. When the doctor examined her, he realized that she was two months pregnant. After treating her, Dr. Robert Smythe told the police that Frances should ride back to jail on the hood of the car. While the police were trying to push Frances onto the hood, Dr. Smythe and several other white doctors and nurses sanctioned this act with their laughter. When the police started to threaten to rape Frances, she fell unconscious. She was then driven back to jail inside the car.

The following morning, Frances was still in need of medical attention. A fellow companion called to a lawyer from the jail window. Finally Charles Evers and Mrs. Reed of the Freedom Democratic Party managed to get Frances out of jail. She was taken to a black doctor and told that she had received poor medical attention. This incident was reported to the FBI and Frances pointed out the policemen who beat her. Two months later the FBI dropped the case because they said they did not have enough witnesses. Frances believes that one result of the investigation was that Dr. Smythe at the hospital was fired.

Frances' civil rights activity and her consultation with the FDP and the FBI is on her medical chart at University Hospital. The first time Frances returned to University Hospital after this incident, a nurse badgered her about this information on her chart. Nurses and doctors in emergency have told her, "What good did it do you to go to the FBI?" On other occasions she has simply been refused medical attention.

This past school year, Mrs. Porter's daughter, Frankie Mae (ten years old), experienced a great amount of difficulty as a student at a formerly all-white school. The school is still predominantly white with a smattering of black children. Frankie Mae was the only black child in her class and as a result was subjected to harsh emotional and physical brutality.

When Frankie Mae was involved with a white child in any incident, she was "whipped" by the white teacher (or the teacher's husband). Frankie Mae's desk was placed in a corner which isolated her from the rest of the white class. Mrs. P. became aware of her daughter's treatment when she noticed that Frankie Mae would come home every day with her hair washed. Although Mrs. P. would fix Frankie Mae's hair in the morning, the teacher would wash it because Frankie Mae's hair bothered her white classmates. Finally, the school officials tried to persuade Mrs. Porter to transfer Frankie Mae to the "Negro" school. Mrs. Porter refused because the school Frankie Mae was now attending was closer to her home than the "Negro" school. The school's next tactic was to demand that Frankie Mae be removed to the "Negro" school because she was psychotic. When Mrs. Porter refused to take Frankie Mae to the psychiatrist, the school tried to get the welfare department to request the change in schools. Although the welfare department requested a transfer, it did not go through for some reason. In the end, the schools got their way because Mrs. Porter moved into another school district.

## Life at Home

When confronted with the living conditions of the Porter family, one wonders if this is really 1971 in the richest country in the world. Eleven members of the family live in a three-room shotgun apartment (a rectangular, one-story building with two apartments separated by a common wall; the rooms in each apartment are placed one behind the other). There is a double bed and a few chairs in the living room. A twin bed and two rollaway beds are in the next room.

(When the beds are all open, there is barely room to walk.) A sink and stove complete the kitchen. There is neither a refrigerator nor a kitchen table. The children sit on the floor to eat their meals. Although there is an indoor toilet, the plumbing is defective. The toilet waste remains under the house and frequently washes into the yard. Most of the windowpanes are missing. Mrs. Porter says that she does not know what she is going to do when it gets cold. The landlord keeps promising to fix it, but nothing is ever done. In addition, there is no hot water. The rent is $7 a week.

Mrs. Porter receives $65 per month from the department of welfare. She spends from $25 to $30 a month on food. She buys all of her food from the local grocery; she knows that the prices are higher but this is the only place that will give her credit. At present she is in debt to the grocer for $24. Her other debts are as follows:

telephone $15
utilities $10
one pair of eyeglasses $13 (original cost $40)
shoes $21.30 (original cost $30 for 4 pairs)
University Hospital—$130 for birth of granddaughter

Recently, she bought a secondhand refrigerator. The price was $114 with no money down. After paying $10 toward her bill, she realized that the refrigerator was broken—"it kept defrosting." The company took the refrigerator back and Mrs. P. lost her $10.

The family's diet consists primarily of surplus commodities and food bought on credit. The family eats only two meals a day: hotcakes and syrup for breakfast and soup and corn bread for dinner. Although a good portion of the commodities are spoiled, Mrs. Porter makes good use out of what is salvageable. The pancakes and bread are made from the commodity flour and the commodity meat is eaten until it is gone. The children will not drink the surplus dry milk, but Mrs. Porter uses it in her cooking. The children go without whole milk.

Although brief, I believe that the above study of the Porter family exemplifies the conditions of racism, poverty and injustice in Mississippi.

## STUDY QUESTIONS

1. Study the Face Sheet data. Without reading the narrative, what picture do you get of the Porter family situation? Could you tell, for example, whether the family was white or black?

2. Do you feel the action of leaving town at night to avoid paying their debts was a responsible or irresponsible act? Explain.

3. Mrs. Porter did not go to school until she was twelve years old. (The State of Mississippi has no law requiring compulsory school attendance.) Why do you think the state has not passed such a seemingly reasonable law, even in 1971?

4. If Mr. Porter was a "very mean man," why did Mrs. P. choose to live with him for seventeen years?

5. How would you account for Mrs. P.'s three miscarriages and one stillbirth? Poor hospital care? Poor nutrition? Would it be likely or unlikely for a poor white Mississippian to have a similar record of difficulty? Why?

6. If the national minimum wage is $1.60 an hour, how can Mrs. Porter get only $3 a day for domestic work or picking cotton?

7. In Mrs. P.'s subsequent repeated attempts to get public assistance, do you think she would have been more successful if she had been part of a black welfare rights organization (than as an individual with the help of a sympathetic white man) ?

8. If the person handing out NAACP leaflets had been a local, poor white, do you think she would have been treated differently by the police? How about a northern white? A northern black?

9. Why is it unlikely that Mrs. P. will be successful in her lawsuit against the Negro policeman, even with witnesses? Would she stand a greater chance of being successful if she appealed the case up to the State Supreme Court? Explain your answer.

10. Given the situation with her daughter Carrie, would you agree that the decision for her sterilization was a proper one?

11. If Mrs. P. had come to you as her worker at the local antipoverty agency, what would you have done—and what would you have advised her to do—in regard to the situation with Mr. Cameron and Idela?

12. Could the incident of Frances with the police and hospital personnel have occurred outside Mississippi—for example, in a city up North?

13. Why would the FBI drop a case like Idela's if she was prepared to make sworn testimony, had eyewitnesses, and corroborating medical evidence?

14. If you were a medical social worker and knew that her civil rights activity was on her medical records, what would you do about the situation? What do you feel would be your most effective approach in such an instance? Why?

15. If you were a school social worker and knew that Frankie Mae was unjustly being declared psychotic so that she could be transferred against her will, what would you do about the situation? What would be your most effective approach in such an instance? Why?

16. What do you think of the way in which Mrs. P. handled her budget? If you were Mrs. P., living in her situation, what would you do differently?

17. If the surplus food (commodities) are certified by the U.S. Department of Agriculture and sealed under government inspection, how could "a good portion of them be spoiled"?

18. Does the Porter Family Social Study differ radically from the case records which graduate social work students normally study? Are cases like the Porter Social Study rele-

vant for students who are going to practice in a northern or an urban setting? Explain.

19. How would you assess the ego strengths of Mrs. Porter? What is the nature of the pathology? Could you make a preliminary psychosocial diagnosis? What would be an appropriate treatment intervention?

# The Case of Mrs. Susie T.

Ronald M. Arundell

On the morning of June 13, I received a call from the pastor of Ramsen Baptist Church in Jackson. He asked if we could assist him in helping Mrs. T. (one of his parishioners) who was undergoing labor pains. He explained that she had been refused admission to the hospital because she had no money. I got the address and said that I would see her immediately. There was to be a twofold plan: 1) to get her examined at University Medical Center and make arrangements for her upcoming delivery; and 2) to go to the welfare department to file an application for ADC.

I then went to her home to see what I could do to assist. I knocked, and after I had explained that her pastor had sent me, Mrs. T.'s mother invited me in. Mrs. T. was lying on the bed and she was in pain. After seeing her condition I said, "Let's go to the hospital and we can talk on the way." As we drove, Mrs. T. gave me the following information:

Mrs. T. was a twenty-eight-year-old black woman. She had six children ranging from two to twelve years of age. Her husband had left her about four months ago and she believed that he had gone North to find work. She had not heard from him since then. She had no money and her children had not eaten in two days. Her rent was overdue and she was afraid that she would be evicted. Her mother had been helping her with the family, but her mother did not have much money either. When I asked her if she had applied for welfare, she said that she went there a year ago but they had said that she was not eligible.

Mrs. T. seemed to have a great deal of strength. Although she cried at times, this was normal for the situation. She was not hysterical and was able to understand things without too much trouble. I engaged her in conversation as we rode in the car and tried to relax her by explaining that I was a social work student from New York down for the summer.

## The Hospital Experience

We arrived at the University Hospital and went to the emergency room. There I told the Charge Nurse that Mrs. T. was having labor pains and asked that she be immediately examined. She was examined by a doctor who gave her a pill to take as he filled out a clinic appointment for June 19 at 10:30 A.M. The doctor explained that they were false labor pains but she was due any day. If she felt the baby was coming he said she should return to the hospital and she would be admitted to delivery if she had $100. This is the charge for those who are medically indigent. Mrs. T. explained to me that she hadn't a cent to her name and she began to cry saying, "What am I going to do?" The doctor said, "That's your problem. Nothing is given for free in this world."

I told Mrs. T. to sit down in the lobby and I would look into this situation.

I immediately called the Schwerner Fund's Project Coordinator in order to find out the policy of this hospital. Coming from an area that had free clinics for those who could not pay I naïvely believed that this hospital could not refuse to assist a person in need of medical service simply because she could not pay. But as I found out, I was wrong. You had to have $100 to have a baby.

I went first to see Miss Crossman, ACSW, Supervisor of Medical Social Work, University Medical Center. I was granted an interview and I explained to her that Mrs. T., a client of mine, had just been examined in the emergency room. I explained that unless she had $100 they would refuse to treat her. I stressed that this must be some sort of mistake.

Miss Crossman explained that it was the policy of the hospital to charge a fee for all obstetrical patients. This hospital, she went on, is trying to develop a meaningful prenatal program. Thus, a woman is required to begin the program when she first realizes that she is pregnant. She comes weekly to the clinic. A plan is worked out whereby she pays so much a week or month so that the $100 is paid by the time she has to deliver.

I said that Mrs. T. did not have the money for such a program. For the last seven months she has been destitute. Her husband deserted her.

Miss Crossman pointed out that she should have come earlier to this program or have gone to the Department of Health where they could have helped her. She waited until the last minute and then expects to have her baby without paying.

I said Mrs. T. did not know about the Department of Health programs.

Miss Crossman said, "Well, she should have known."

I then became very angry. I said, "As a social worker you should know about the alienation of the poor; their lack of knowledge of the services; the difficulty they have getting to the Department of Health and even to University Hospital."

Miss Crossman said, "You don't have to lecture me."

I replied, "But what is she to do? Are you going to turn her away? Is she to have her child in the streets?"

Miss Crossman replied, "She can use a midwife."

I said, "A what?"

"A midwife. This is a way for her to have her child. It is

done all over the world. It is also an accepted method in this state."

I said, "In America there is no excuse for such a thing. Midwives are nineteenth-century stuff. Every person has a right to medical help."

Miss Crossman then proceeded to explain the wonderful benefits of a midwife. I could no longer stand this and said, "I never heard so much bull in my life."

Miss Crossman then said that $100 was the policy of the hospital. She had nothing to do with this policy. I asked her how as a social worker she could tolerate such a system. Miss Crossman's reply: "You know that as a social worker, one has a commitment to the agency."

I had heard this phrase used many times. I got up and left the room.

I then proceeded to see Mrs. McCleary who is in charge of the clinic. I explained the situation to her. She coldly responded that everyone has to pay $100. There are no exceptions. She said also that it is not *her* problem that my client does not have the money.

I said to Mrs. McC., "Do you realize how hard it is to save $100 when you have no money?"

She said, "I am sorry about that. She has to have $100 or she can go somewhere else."

I really tore into her then. I said, "This hospital is the worst thing that I have seen in my life." I told her that I was going to the hospital director to see about this.

I went to see the director, Dr. Green. I walked into his office and said, "I would like to see you, doctor." It caught him off guard. He then heard my problem and said that the administrator of the hospital would be able to help me with this situation. I said that if he did not take care of it, I would be right back.

I then saw Mr. Thompson. He explained to me that the policy of the hospital was that patients were taken for private care when they have their own physician; this was based on the patient's ability to pay for this service. In the case where the patients were in public care, they would come to a clinic. This policy was based on the person's ability to pay.

I reminded him that Mrs. T. had no money.

He said that a program of prenatal care is worked out where a person pays so much a month before delivery so that at the time of the birth when she enters the hospital she will have paid the $100.

I replied, "But, Mrs. T. has been destitute for the last eight months. She has no money. Not $5, $10 or even $1."

He then said that in an emergency medical care cannot be denied because of the lack of money. He went on and seemed to imply that the way to beat the system was to wait until there was an emergency and then bring the woman to the hospital. I said, "I understand that $100 has to be paid after the baby is delivered or else the woman is kept in the hospital until she raises the money." (I had checked this out with the head of the emergency clinic.)

He said, "Well, this isn't always true. The people on the floor sometimes use this approach to get the people to pay." He then began to stall.

I said that Mrs. T. was *destitute*. "She has an appointment at the clinic on Monday. She is broke. She will apply for welfare. What are you going to do about taking care of her?"

He then said, "There is no such thing as free medical care. Someone has to pay for it. In her case, it seems that the State of Mississippi will. You get a letter from welfare saying that she is destitute and I will make sure that she is taken care of." He took her name and said that he would alert the people in the clinic and administration of her inability to pay.

I told him that I would personally work with Mrs. T. and I expected her to be treated in the proper manner. If she were not, then I would have to file a complaint with HEW.

I then went back to the lobby to see Mrs. T. I informed her that the situation was corrected and that she would not have to pay. I suggested that we now go over to the welfare office and get her on the rolls so that she could get some money for food and rent. She agreed.

## The Welfare Experience

When we arrived at the welfare office, I immediately went to the administrator and told her that I had a woman in labor with me and I expected a quick interview and some money. (I had talked with Mrs. T. before we got there and told her the plan of attack. She began to laugh and said she would go along with it.)

The reason I wanted the process to be hurried is that the normal interview for intake takes one to two hours. The number of forms that have to be filled out are unbelievable. During the interview, I kept harassing the worker. The reason for this was that Mrs. T.'s husband had not been gone from the home for six months. Thus, under Mississippi welfare rules, Mrs. T. would be ineligible for three more months. I explained this to the client beforehand but I wanted to make sure that the worker would not confuse Mrs. T. so that she might "forget" and give the right answer. The most important thing was that Mrs. T. get on the rolls so that she would get some money.

She was accepted. I also got the worker to give Mrs. T. $2 out of her own pocket, provide a slip that would entitle her to $20 worth of food, and another slip of paper to a private social agency who would pay the back rent.

During the interview, I had Mrs. T. groan in order that the worker would think that the baby might be born in her office. The worker was in a cold sweat, and managed to finish the paper work in fifteen minutes.

## Postscript

Mrs. T. finally had a baby boy eight weeks later. She was given free medical service for the delivery and for the six subsequent clinic visits. In addition, she accepted on welfare.

## *Worker's Evaluation*

This was my first encounter with such an archaic system. There was no such thing as free medical service. Over the months, I met a number of black women who had been denied admittance to the hospital because they did not have the money. Two women had to have their children delivered at a midwife's house ten minutes from the hospital. The midwife's (or "granny-lady's") name is Josephine Wilson. I had a number of meetings with her. In 1964 she delivered 117 babies. Four mothers and three children died. The stories that she can document are unbelievable.

One case that Mrs. Wilson related involved a woman who went to the University Hospital in labor. She had no money. She was turned away. There on her kitchen floor, Mrs. Wilson worked to deliver her baby. However, the baby had a "water head" and could not be discharged from the womb without surgery. Mrs. W. called three doctors and the hospital. All refused to come. The woman died on her kitchen floor. The baby had already been dead for two weeks. This is just one case. I was called one evening by Mrs. Wilson and I rushed over to the house of one of her patients. As I arrived, the woman was having her baby. It was one of the most discouraging events of the whole summer. I had arrived too late. This child was born in a roach-infested kitchen because the mother had no money to go to the hospital. The child was born alive and the mother is well today. But the situation remains. No money, no health care.

## STUDY QUESTIONS

1. Do you think Mrs. Crossman's explanation of hospital policy was reasonable or unreasonable? Why did the worker become so angry? Was his anger justified? Functional?

2. "You know as a social worker, one has a commitment to

the agency." What is the worker's commitment to his agency; and what is his commitment to his client? What can he do if his commitments here come into conflict?

3. What do you think of Mr. Thompson's response to the worker? Do you think his approach was reasonable?

4. Should the worker have encouraged Mrs. T. to lie to the welfare intake investigator? What is his responsibility to a public agency?

5. Midwives are an accepted method of care in Mississippi (and in many European countries as well). Under these circumstances, should the worker be so upset by the prospect of Mrs. T. having her child delivered by midwife? How much of his reaction can be accounted for by his lack of familiarity with state and local customs?

6. What about the worker's handling of Mrs. T.? What more could he have done in this situation to handle her feelings?

7. How does the worker convince his client that he is not "selling her out," while he effectively uses manipulation as a method to obtain the service she needs?

8. Is this proper work for an *organizer*? Do individual cases aid in the organizer's task of establishing a welfare rights organization?

*PART IV*

# PRACTICE
# DILEMMAS

# A Season in Mississippi: Vignettes From a Black Volunteer

JUDITH BEYMAN

Upon first arrival in Mississippi, it reminds one of any suburban community. But one soon realizes that this is hostile territory.

I arrived in Jackson on a Friday, and was soon on my way to a welfare rights meeting in Morningstar, a small community outside of Jackson. I drove up to an empty church building. However, there was no meeting. Mr. Jones, the chairman of the welfare rights group in this community, soon came up the road to tell us that this was revival time. People spent most of their time in church, leaving no time to come to meetings. It soon became obvious that Mr. Jones had not informed anyone of this meeting because of his fear of retaliation from the white community. Later, the chairman of the county's Welfare Rights Movement confirmed this. She thought that somebody had "spoken" with Mr. Jones.

Ironically, amidst all of this fear, the white power structure expected a riot on Monday. On that day, people throughout

Adapted with permission of the Association of Black Social Workers from *Black Caucus,* Vol. 1, No. 1 (Fall, 1968), pp. 49–58.

the state congregated in Jackson and walked to the capital to demonstrate that people were starving in Mississippi. The "Poor People's March" was surrounded by numerous Jackson police and highway patrolmen.

As a black Northerner, I questioned the effectiveness of the march. I saw poor black mothers, children, crippled adults and the aged marching in the hot Jackson sun. Many had to leave at 3:00 A.M. to arrive in Jackson by 10:00 A.M. These people had been motivated to come this far to march. They applauded Charles Evers when he called the Governor a liar on the grounds outside the capitol. They agreed with him when he denounced the idea that black Mississippians were going to riot. In these people's eyes, Charles Evers was probably the most courageous black man that they had ever met.

Community organization here is different from its northern variety. Public marches seem to be needed to whip up enthusiasm and encourage the people to continue to press for their rights. To those black marchers, they were the courageous people in Mississippi. To me, it seemed as if nothing concrete had been gained—but this was not the opinion of the majority.

## Differences: North and South

I soon realized that there were many different aspects to black southern community organization. The pervasive fear, the need for demonstrations such as the Poor People's March to drum up community spirit, the need for more familiar (closer) relationships between the community organizer and the community, and the strong religious beliefs of the people which transcend every aspect of the community's life are met with a greater intensity here than in the North. The people spent the first half hour of the meeting praying: opening song, opening reading from the Bible, another song, an impromptu prayer, and so forth. Even one of the most intelligent leaders of one of the welfare rights group spoke of seeing "visions." (I've met this in the North but these people were usually not leaders.) *The volunteer had to understand and respect this way of life to be effective.*

Meeting the institutions of white racism was another earth-shaking experience. There is no free medical care in Mississippi. The University Hospital—the only quasi-public hospital in Mississippi—charges a fee of $8 for a metal plate (clinic card) and $2 every time you visit the clinic. The Welfare Rights Movement was successful in getting a few of its clients free medical care by advising the hospital to bill the patient and then informing the patient not to pay. To make certain that they were not billed, I drove the Porter family to the hospital in time for their 7:30 A.M. appointment and remained with them until everyone was examined. (For details see "The Porter Family Social Study".) Typical of most black children I saw in Mississippi, the Porter children were thin; they had open running sores on their limbs and also worms.

The building of the University Hospital may exemplify the 1960's but the treatment of black clients is "pre-60." The patient must first meet the white bitches at the desk who demand money or no service, and call black people by their first names. You look around and see the black child with no nose and the scores of people with gross physical defects—including severe burns and missing limbs. After you enter the clinic and sit down, you suddenly realize that white people sit on one side of the waiting room and black on the other. You look upon the wall and see that the WHITE and COLORED signs have been removed. The white hospital social worker assures me that it is voluntary segregation. But you see the reaction on the part of the white patients and white staff when you and the Porter family sit on the "white" side.

## Welfare Rights

The southern department of welfare is an affront to the federal social welfare law. The welfare clients want the Welfare Rights Organization to represent them when applying for welfare because they have been turned away all too often, or have had to submit to intensive questions about their sexual habits. (I believe that the mysticism surrounding sex and racism in the South continues to foster segregation of the races.) The white bitches in the welfare department receive their vicarious thrills through their rather warped questioning about the sex life of ADC mothers. I learned a lot from these interviews. For example, a man with a metal plate in his head had worked as a field hand for ten years despite the fact that he frequently passed out on the job. This same man was raising two children in a home without running water, heat or electricity. He used kerosene lamps and he had to obtain water from a neighbor's well. This man had not realized that he qualified for APTD (Aid to the Permanently and Totally Disabled) until we met him at a welfare rights meeting.

The growth and strength of these welfare rights organizations are the only thing—other than a revolution—that will help these people. The groups are growing and abuses will decrease as the people learn their rights and exercise them.

## STUDY QUESTIONS

1. The writer said she "questioned the effectiveness" of the march. Was it the march's effectiveness she was questioning —or was it something else?

2. What does Beyman mean when she says, "Community organization here is different from its northern variety"?

3. "The volunteer had to understand and respect this way of life to be effective." Do you agree? Or could either understanding or respect be sufficient for the committed volunteer?

4. Is it ethical for a professional social worker to advise clients to tell the hospital to bill them for services—and then privately tell the client to feel free to do this, knowing she will not (and cannot) pay the bill?

5. Do you think the white hospital staff might have reacted differently to Mrs. Porter's sitting on the "white" side of the waiting room if the worker (also black) had not been with her? Why would it make any difference (since both worker *and* client are black)?

6. What does Beyman mean when she says, "I believe that the mysticism surrounding sex and racism in the South continues to foster segregation of the races"?

7. "The growth and strength of welfare rights organizations are the only thing—other than a revolution—that will help these people." Do you agree? Are there other (third) solutions?

# Excerpts From the Log of a Summer Volunteer

HEATHER SMITH

*July 15*

Schedule: 9:30 A.M. to CDA (Community Development Agency—the action arm of the Michael Schwerner Fund in Mississippi) for meeting with Gerry and Jesse. They are the indigenous staff of CDA in Jackson. Arranged to have a staff meeting on Wednesday evening. 11:00—to Federation of Settlement Houses office to meet the Director re: placements in small town of Utica. 12:30—went to meet Rev. Smith re: NYC (Neighborhood Youth Corps) in Utica.

The NYC kids can be used for almost any productive purpose and this opens up possibilities for us. I would like to see them develop their own project, hopefully adding to the organizational efforts. There can be as many as forty NYC kids. Complicating the registration procedure is the fact that

This excerpt from Miss Smith's log deals mainly with her experiences with teen-agers hired by the Neighborhood Youth Corps in a rural town in central Mississippi. Reference is made to "John," who is John Hickey, then a student at the School of Social Work, University of Maryland, Baltimore, Md. Mr. Hickey is presently a Social Work Officer, Medical Service Corps, United States Army.

the kids and their parents will have to come all the way from the rurals of Utica into Jackson to fill out the application. This means a major transportation job. There is no public transportation from the rurals into Jackson.

Something which upset me today was my first meeting with clients. I was awed by the strength of these people. My life and its struggles seem dwarfed by the sheer fact that they have survived in the face of such odds. Mrs. Carroll takes care of three small children on the starvation allowance of welfare. In her front room, which of necessity contains a bed, there are large water stains on the ceiling. The back yard is strung with laundry, clearly a morning's undertaking. Yet the yard blooms with flowers and she speaks of canvassing the neighborhood to revive the welfare rights group. When Gerry urged her to do this my inner feeling was to offer to help her accomplish this task out of my feeling of guilt for my youth and energy and time. And I recognize that I have done too much in the past for the groups I have worked with, out of the same feelings.

*July 17*
Met NYC kids at Strawbridge, 10:00. To Jackson to sign kids up. Back to Utica taking kids home. (Strawbridge and Utica are towns in rural areas of Hinds County. Jackson is the major city, state capital and county seat.)

There was a mix-up at the Community Service Association and we were told by the receptionist that there were no more NYC slots open. We waited for Mr. A. to come back from lunch to straighten this out. When he came, he accepted the kids' applications. I advised the receptionist that anyone from Utica was to be accepted. During my waiting around, a couple of the white secretaries mentioned that they knew white kids in Utica who needed jobs. I discouraged them, feeling that integrating this project would be more of a detriment than anything else.

After the kids had been processed, while they were together in a group waiting to go home, I said that I would credit them with two hours of work for every eligible person they brought on Friday. There was immediate enthusiasm among the girls and I made a point to ask the boys to find more guys. They nodded silently. I also plan to give credit to the girls who volunteered to get the key for the church and try to find a more convenient meeting place. I'm doing this not only to get the jobs done, but because I don't want to exploit these kids and I feel they should be paid for work performed.

*July 19*

10:00—Strawbridge 12:00—To Mrs. J. and then Mrs. W. re: APTD (Aid to the Permanently and Totally Disabled) application.

At Strawbridge today my strategy for recruiting kids worked to the tune of twenty-six new applicants. The church was almost full of kids and parents. We outlined the program and what the procedure was for processing. We didn't offer transportation. I felt the crowd responded to my talk—I got laughter at my humor and I felt I might be getting through and not just being a white face. At one point when I was speaking about the purpose of the project and what the kids would be doing, I said that we knew that the people here had welfare problems. A chorus of mothers from the front row responded, "Yessum"—and food stamp problems— "That's the truth!"—and social security problems—"Sho' nuff," etc. For a moment I felt what it was like to be a preacher; the rhythm of the thing was powerful and it was only because I was embarrassed and self-conscious that I stopped.

Only four kids said they could get into Jackson that day but we let the rest go to find their own way, passing out the names and addresses of the places to go. When discussing the possibility of getting another church, the group of women who had been my chorus said that was unlikely, since only Reverend Smith had the nerve to open his church for functions like this. Mrs. J. who is a member of the board of the church said that during the boycott Reverend Smith had moved to this church because the church he had been in refused to have the meetings any more for fear of being burned down. She said that they weren't afraid to be burned —they'd just build again. As it turned out, the only action the white community had taken was to put tacks on the road. We laughed at the foolishness of the white men throwing away good tacks and how the tacks had been swept up and used.

Mrs. J. seems to be full of get up and go. She is a grand-mother, having raised ten children. She and her husband worked in the cotton fields for many years and made next to nothing. They were able to get a loan and buy the five acres and the house they now live in. By raising their own cotton they were able to pay off the loan in two years. When she heard about the NYC program she went out recruiting kids. I have a feeling that she is a good potential organizer. We went with her to see her husband's sister, Mrs. W.

Mrs. W. is sixty-four, white-haired and thin. She lives down a dirt road in a house without water, electricity or gas. She chops and hauls wood to cook and heat with, and she hauls all her water from a well that is a good distance from the house. Her daughter and her five children live with Mrs. W. and her other daughter, who lives a few houses down, leaves her seven children during the day for which she gives her mother a dollar a week. The house has no more than three rooms. Mrs. W. and all the children were barefoot. She had been turned down last year for APTD although she has a tumor the size of a rubber ball on her left hand and another tumor starting on her right elbow. Her daughter gets $50 per month from ADC for the children and this is the only money coming into the household except for what the other sister donates. We advised Mrs. W. not to say anything about this donation, and also not to say she chopped wood and hauled water. We arranged to come by and take her into Jackson to the welfare office on Tuesday. Mrs. J. was concerned that she might not trust us and Mrs. W. replied that she knew we were "good folks that the Lord had sent to help her." John suggested (as we were walking to the car) that Mrs. W. might like Mrs. J. to go with her on Tuesday. When Mrs. J. called back and asked her, Mrs. W. replied, "No, I ain't afraid." I was again awed and astounded and filled with respect. John says that there is still a chance that she might not go, but I hope that she does because I want to believe in her. It is very frustrating to know that I may never be seen as a person, never be able to relate to her as an equal, always be a "nice white lady"—and this frustration got me down for a while.

*July 24*

There were twenty-two kids at Strawbridge. Mrs. J. volunteered to take a group in to register and I advised them not to be turned away—to sit there all day and make a fuss if they were given a run-around. I was frustrated that I could not be in both places and frustrated that I had no power or influence and I'm sure this showed. But my concern and my placing the *kids'* welfare first also showed through as I later learned from Mrs. J., who relishes retelling the story of how I told them to just sit there, with obvious pleasure at being given the chance to hassle the system. I also knew from listening around at the NYC office that "grass-rootsy" folks who don't take no for an answer are respected and responded to.

We discussed the survey with the kids and formulated a list of questions—it was difficult getting most of the kids to participate in this; we have many quiet ones.

*July 26*

There were thirty kids at Strawbridge. The difficulties with registration seem to have cleared up but some kids were discouraged. We distributed the surveys and talked about interviewing. The kids left early with the understanding that sometime over the weekend they would put in the hours necessary to get the surveys filled out. We divided them into teams of two and gave each team twelve copies. A local black social worker contends that we won't get many back. I have no way of checking up on or supervising the kids in their surveying; I have to trust them.

*July 29*

There were thirty-one kids at Strawbridge. We got 150 filled-in surveys back! The kids participated in tallying the results and a list of the priority needs was put on the blackboard. The kids discussed what they could do and voted to focus their efforts on food stamps.

*July 31*

There were thirty-six kids at Strawbridge. We distributed the budget forms and began training in their use and in food stamp regulations. There is confusion over the math necessary. It is difficult to work with such a large group, especially when we don't really know the kids. They are reluctant to reveal their inabilities and so many are quiet. I am reluctant to use the traditional methods of teaching. I feel that calling on individuals for answers to problems would embarrass and discourage them more than benefit. John tried dividing them into pairs and having them teach each other, but I don't think the results were very good—in too many cases it was the blind leading the blind. We don't know them well enough to pick out those who are competent.

*August 2*

The budget training continues. I have taken the lead in this. Divided the kids into four groups of nine each with a leader chosen by the kids. I broke the form down into problems and had the groups competing with each other on solutions of various examples of these problems. The groups could compare notes internally. They had to decide on the one answer they thought correct and if it was right, they got 9 points. This way, the more skilled would teach the less skilled and we never had to locate the skilled; their status was derived from the group, and we never forced the kids to expose to *us* their limitations. We kept score on the board and there was a great deal of enthusiasm and competition engendered. The day ended with everyone in high spirits—including me. I felt that this was the first time the kids had been able to enjoy themselves with us. It was a fun day. I told the kids we would continue with the competition and that we'd arrange for a treat for the winners. We encouraged the kids to practice with their parents and friends at home.

*August 5*

Four parents were asked to act as sample interviewees for a couple of kids from each group to interview. Each group therefore got to interview each parent and eight of the nine kids in each group got to conduct an interview. We had the parents get their stories together before we started so that they would be comparable and so that we could get the facts for a check, and so that we could give them a gimmick—example, give their income in weekly figures so the kids would have to figure the monthly amount; give medical expenses only for self unless asked specifically for the rest of the family, etc. Some of the parents' own stories were so good they didn't need any addition. It was a hectic and busy day for all and the parents got a good deal of pleasure from participating.

The results of this "test" were not good. There is a great deal of trouble with basic math. The kids are still not asking enough questions, obviously sticking pretty much to the form and not getting to know the interviewee. James S., the Dudley brothers and Canuary F. are the most competent at this point. I spent a *great* deal of time correcting their work, analyzing the mistakes and writing suggestions. I don't think any teacher ever spent so much effort on any test.

*August 6*

We were invited to the Morningstar meeting to help with food stamp budgets. James, the Dudley brothers, Daisy S. and a couple of other kids went to the meeting for that purpose. The adults were not enthusiastic about the kids doing this. In fact, one lady approached John and me before the meeting when we were talking to James, and asked if *we* would help her with her food stamps. John turned to James and said that he was trained to do this and would be glad to help her. She continued to talk to John and when he constantly relayed her questions to James, she finally went inside to the meeting room. There were only a few people at the meeting but there was a good deal of productive talk about ways of getting things changed and the kids did figure out a number of budgets (with a good deal of help from us) and arranged to go to Jackson on Thursday with a couple of women.

*August 7*

From my analysis of the sample budgets, I had isolated a few areas of weakness in math and had the groups competing on solution to a battery of examples. Reverend Smith came to this meeting and he addressed the group before it had begun. We expected him to say a few friendly words. Instead he lectured at the group from behind the pulpit for almost forty-five minutes on many subjects including: politics —his running for office, criticizing the community because he had lost the last election; that the group should be grateful for his having gotten them these jobs, against the wishes of the supervisors; and that the group should be thankful that these nice, white people would come here and work with them and that they should be respectful and obedient toward us. By the end of his speech the atmosphere was dead, and the kids were slumped down in their seats looking at the floor, fidgeting, etc. John and I were uncomfortable and embarrassed. We called a break and had a chance to talk to Reverend Smith. It seems that he has had some of the kids in his classes at Dixon Jr. High and considers some of them troublemakers—especially the Jones brothers. I assured him that they had been no trouble to us and communicated my embarrassment at his lecturing. This made little impression.

During the time spent on the math problems, Reverend Smith again "volunteered his services." He took the blackboard for a few minutes to throw out a couple of trick problems for the group to solve: What is one-half of XII? there are two answers, 6 and VII (erasing the lower half of XII). The kids gave him both answers and he was fooled. Then he asked them to do a multiplication problem in base 8 (new math, which the kids have never had). Willie Jones volunteered to do it and did it in regular math. Reverend Smith took full advantage of the opportunity to put him down and then briefly (and unsatisfactorily) explained the correct answer. He was obviously stuffing his own ego at the expense of these kids, and I was furious. Because of his influential position, though, I was afraid to say much in the way of consolation after he had gone.

*August 8*

Spent the day in the welfare office with two clients and James S. James was a great help in the interviews with clients, and by the end of the day he was harassing the food stamp workers with questions about food stamp law which we had been wondering about in the training sessions. I am acutely aware of our lack of knowledge in this area and am constantly wishing that Gerry were around to answer questions. Volunteers should really be thoroughly briefed in welfare and food stamp law so that they can be more effective. It is really not enough to be a white face. (And, as John found out, it can be very detrimental to a female black client to have a white male advocate.)

*August 9*

Gerry came out to Strawbridge to help with training the kids and we did a lot of role playing. She was a hit with the kids. And James told the group about his experiences at the welfare office.

Went to a client's house with Ernest Dudley to figure a budget but found that the income was from cotton and we couldn't figure it without the bills, which she would get; and more knowledge which we hoped we could get.

Gerry had spoken to a welfare worker about smuggling the food stamp manual out for us. We stopped by her house to arrange for this. She is a charming and liberal gal, and she and Gerry have a good working relationship. She'll get the manual for us on Monday but we'll have to copy it and get it back to her by Tuesday.

## August 12

The food stamp trailer comes to Utica tomorrow and we discussed our plans. The kids had been asked to return to some of the families they interviewed who had mentioned food stamp problems, and work out budgets so that they could accompany them in interviews at the trailer. No one had been able to do this—some claimed they hadn't been able to catch anyone at home; some said the families didn't want their help. We arranged to meet at the trailer, anyway, and get clients off the lines.

## August 13

John went out to the food stamp trailer in Utica while I stayed behind and Xeroxed the food stamp manual at LCDC (Lawyers' Committee for Constitutional Defense). At about 1:00 the lawyers received a call from John about trouble at the trailer—they had been refused entrance—and I was frustrated and on edge until John got back and related the story. The kids had gotten there early and interviewed people in the line, making out budgets and asking if people wanted them to accompany them in the interview. The response from the clients was good—they were glad to get help and were willing to say that they wanted the kids with them. By the time the trailer opened the kids were well prepared and the first few people had kids with them. James and his client were first in line and he got in to the interview even though questioned at the door. He replied that the client had a right to representation and the client said she wished him to accompany her. It was probably more of the surprise factor that got him in. The next in line was Linda, basically a quiet girl, whom we did not know too much about. When she attempted to enter the trailer with her client, the worker stood in her way and refused to let her enter. Although she said the same things that James had, the worker would not back down and tried to shut the door on her. When this failed, he called one of the white workmen who help set up the trailer. He then mounted the stairs and was about to push her down forcibly when John intervened and called her down. She would not have budged without this word from John. The kids withdrew to the background to discuss what to do, and John and a couple of the kids went to call LCDC for advice. LCDC said go to the "higher-ups" in Jackson. The group planned to give it another try the following morning; and, if refused entrance, to have enough cars there to make the trip to Jackson.

*August 14*

Essentially the same scene took place this morning, except that it was briefer, the workers being prepared for it, and we prepared to leave. Thirteen kids were piled into three cars and we convened at the welfare department in Jackson. During the trip we discussed the events and the strategy of confronting the welfare department. We discussed the various run-arounds they might get from secretaries, receptionists, etc., and the final resource of going over the supervisor's head to the Agriculture Department. The kids were in high spirits by the time we arrived, ready to testify and make their demands. When they asked for Mrs. D., the supervisor, the receptionist said she wasn't available at that time and the kids told her that they would then see the head of the food stamp program, and that they would wait. They stood in a body at the receptionist's desk. She excused herself and scurried away. Within a few minutes Mrs. D. appeared to ask what the trouble was. She met with the kids in the waiting room of the food stamp section, with row upon row of black clients to witness the confrontation. The kids told her in no uncertain terms what the clients' rights were and that the workers in the trailer had violated these rights. They gave descriptions of how Linda had been "manhandled." Mrs. D. tried to insist that they had no right in the interview. When she said they didn't know enough about it to help, they assured her they'd been trained. She then tried the line, "I've known you all since you were little kids." That just made the group mad—she assumed they were all from welfare families, which was not the case. By this point some of the waiting clients joined in with expressions of support for the kids and even joined in to further the argument. Mrs. D. made the mistake of using the word "nigger" and the group moved closer around her and Ida went into action with a lecture on the use of the word "nigger" and how she was not ever to say that to them again. Mrs. D. was visibly shaken.

When I finally saw that the drama of the moment had been spent and that further confrontation was useless, I passed the word to one of the kids to tell her we were going over her head, and to leave. This was done and the group turned on their heels and stormed out. One client who had witnessed the confrontation followed us out and congratu- lated the kids and told them to come back soon. The whole waiting room had benefited from this happening and the mood was electric and jubilant.

We stopped for lunch between the two offices and by the time we got to the Agriculture Department the kids were a bit spent. Mr. S., the local director, invited all of the kids into his office, found chairs for almost everyone and politely began by giving a monologue on the functioning of the Agriculture Department in the food stamp program. I was afraid it would turn the kids off completely, but they persisted and did get their problems told. Mr. S. hemmed and hawed in a polite, bureaucratic fashion. I was impressed that the kids pressed him for a definite commitment on their being allowed in. During the conversation he received a call from Mrs. D. at the welfare office, and asked the kids if he should talk to her now. They said yes and then sat and listened to his end of it. (I'm sure this was staged for their benefit.) We finally left with really no firm commitment, but I was quite pleased during the ride home that the kids had not been fooled by his "cool" and knew that he hadn't said anything.

*August 16*

The thirteen kids who had gone to Jackson told their experience to the rest of the group. I got them all up front in a group to do this, having seen that individually they are not good at speaking to groups. This worked quite well and kids were competing to get their two-cents in. We suggested that a letter be written in order to further pressure the system, and we discussed who it should be sent to and why it might be effective. The kids composed the letter and asked me to take it home and type it.

*August 19*

John and I were late getting out to Strawbridge and we met the kids coming back from the church on the road. We pulled over to the shoulder and so did they, and they all gathered around to sign the letter and the five copies. It only took about ten minutes for the cops to drive by. Then they drove by in the other direction. By that time we were finished and we left. John and I drove out of town trailed by a cop, and when we got to Raymond there was a cop in the square watching for us. It was a nerve-racking journey.

We had discussed with the kids the possible repercussions of signing the letter. There was some discussion of who could be evicted from their houses, cut off welfare, etc. Only Canuary was reluctant to sign it, but she said no, that she would sign with everyone else. During the discussion it became clear that there were greater issues at stake—pride, dignity, self-worth, or something of that ilk. My awe of these kids grows daily.

*August 23*

We planned for the coming of the food stamp trailer on Monday.

*August 26*

Everyone assembled at the trailer early and interviewed clients. All the clients were aware of what had happened last time and there was a feeling of expectancy in the crowd. One of the clients had to go back home and get bills to justify her expenses, so I took off with her and her NYC worker to get them. By the time I returned, the trailer had opened and the kids had gotten in with no fuss from the workers. The victory had registered on all there, kids and adults alike. There was significant help given by a number of the kids—one woman's stamp price was cut in half. There had been some discussion inside the trailer of the kids' right to be there, but the workers picked Ida to harass, and she wound up harassing them more. They had wanted to have the kids keep quiet and save their questions for the end of the interview, but the kids didn't.

Many of the kids had not picked up a client and some were through with their interviews so they decided to start for home. Shortly thereafter a cop arrived and went inside the trailer. He approached John and me about ten minutes later, asked for our identification, and questioned us as to what we were doing there and what right we had to be there. (My knees were shaking and I was very glad John was there.) Mrs. D., a client whom we had been talking to when the cop approached, helped out also, but the cop almost ignored her. A couple of the kids came over to join in and I felt bad about the fact that the cop got their identification. We must have argued for about twenty minutes about our business there and the legality of it, and the fact we had seen the officials in Jackson. The kids participated freely in this discussion. The cop was not nasty but he didn't want to give in. He claimed it was private property (Mrs. D. later found out he, the cop, owned it!). We finally compromised. He allowed those kids who still had clients and were waiting for interviews to stay, with Mrs. D. to bring them home. This was an important victory. During the time that the cop was dealing with us, the food stamp people had gone to lunch. I am sure they expected that when they returned there would be no kids there. But, although John and I were gone, and the crowd diminished, the representatives would still be in those interviews, *with the tacit approval of the cops*. We checked with Mrs. D. later to see if all went well and it did—there were no further incidents.

*August 28*

This was the last day for the NYC kids. NYC had sent out a form for the kids to fill out evaluating the program, and one for John and me to do on each kid. We found the form so demeaning that we didn't use many of the questions and wound up discussing the values underlying the form with the kids and the values *we* had. We spoke with each one individually—John with the boys and I with the girls—and discussed their achievements and their strengths and weaknesses. Some of this was quite difficult because we did not really know the kids; this was the first one-to-one contact we had had with many of them. It was surprising how much we got to know these kids in that brief contact, and I wished it had occurred at the beginning of the summer. If NYC would only let their supervisors fill out their application forms *this* would provide for initial contact. I am sure that there was a lot of conning done in these brief evaluation sessions and some were useless. It was, however, better than just filling out the forms. Next time though I would have group evaluations, with the kids participating in evaluating each other.

## Feedback about the Project from the Community

The adults came frequently in the beginning and tapered off during the latter part of the summer. Reason: at first they didn't trust us with their kids, and after the political talk in the beginning were frightened. It was a measure of our acceptance that few adults came toward the end of the summer.

Other NYC projects exploited the kids—had them washing windows, chopping grass, etc. The community was very impressed that our kids were paid to learn something and to help people; and that they could come dressed in their good clothes—which to the last, they did.

And the kids were very *excited* to be involved in "civil rights."

## STUDY QUESTIONS

1. "I was awed by the strength of these people." This is not always the customary reaction of a worker to a welfare client. Do you think the writer's feelings are justified; or are they a bit "romantic"?

2. Do you think the worker was correct in discouraging white youngsters from being included in this Neighborhood Youth Corps (NYC) project? Why?

3. How would you evaluate the worker's handling of herself at the church meeting on July 19th? Would you have handled yourself similarly, or not?

4. "We advised Mrs. W. not to say anything about this donation [from her daughter], and also not to say [to the welfare agents] that she chopped wood and hauled water." Do you feel the worker was justified in making this statement? Is it ethical? Professional?

5. "John says that there is still a chance that she [Mrs. W.] might not go, but I hope that she does because I want to believe in her." What does this say about the organizer's feelings in a work setting? Could these feelings interfere with her performance as a worker? How *does* one handle one's feelings in such a situation?

6. A local black social worker is quoted as saying he

doubted that the youngsters would complete their surveys over the weekend; but they did. Why do you imagine the local worker felt the way he did? In spite of the result, could his feelings have been justified? How do you evaluate the worker's handling of the situation?

7. How would you evaluate the worker's handling of the teaching situation on August 2nd? What group work principles did she employ? What is the importance of blending the intellectual and affective components in a learning situation?

8. Why do you suppose the adults were not at first enthusiastic with having the youngsters help out with food stamp budgets? How do you think John, the worker, handled himself in this situation?

9. Discuss the incident with Reverend Smith on August 7th. Why was he acting that way? Were the worker's fears justified? What are the dynamics of the situation? Was the worker correct in the way she handled herself?

10. "As John found out, it can be very detrimental to a female black client to have a white male advocate." What is the writer trying to say in this statement?

11. What are your reactions to having a welfare agent "smuggle out" the food stamp manual? Is such clandestine activity appropriate for a professional worker? Aren't such government manuals public documents?

12. Was the worker justified in the way he handled the incident on August 13th? Should John (the worker) have intervened and asked Linda to come down? In general, how do you evaluate the worker's handling of the situation?

13. Discuss the confrontation at the welfare center on August 14th. Do you think this was a learning experience for the youngsters? For the other clients in the waiting room? How would you evaluate this scene in terms of the phases and stages of community organization discussed by Solomon, Arundell and Kurzman?

14. How do you evaluate the worker's performance at the confrontation of August 14th? Was she justified in "passing the word" to the youngsters to leave? Why?

15. "The kids composed the letter and asked me to take it home and type it." Was this a legitimate request on the part of the youngsters? Was the worker justified in complying?

16. "My awe of these kids grows daily." Are these emotions appropriate? Are they functional or dysfunctional in the professional work situation?

17. At the food stamp trailer, why did the policeman ignore Mrs. D.?

18. What do you think of the compromise worked out with the policeman? Do you agree that the event turned out to be an important victory? Why?

19. What are your over-all feelings about the experience described in these excerpts from a worker's log? What were the merits and limitations of the experience? What would you have done the same if you had been the worker—and what would you have done differently?

# Reflections on the Southern Way of Life: Notes of a White Volunteer

PAUL A. KURZMAN

I was put into jail once, for one night; and, as I stood considering the walls of solid stone, two or three feet thick, the door of wood and iron, a foot thick, and the iron grating which strained the light, I could not help but being struck with the foolishness of that institution which treated me as if I were mere flesh and blood and bones, to be locked up. . . . I saw that if there was a wall of stone between me and my townsmen, there was a still more difficult one to climb or break through, before *they* could get to be as free as I was. . . .

—HENRY THOREAU
"On the Duty of Civil
Disobedience" (c. 1845)

## Monday

I met Ed (Coordinator of the Schwerner Fund's Community Development Agency in Jackson, Miss.) in the morning, and he showed me a kerosene-soaked cross which had

This paper is excerpted from a northern social worker's tape-recorded comments on a typical week's work as a Schwerner Fund volunteer.

been burned on the lawn of one of the white workers with the Movement. We brought the cross into the office. He also mentioned very casually about some threatening telephone calls that *he* had received and one which his wife had picked up. I had just finished rereading *Three Lives for Mississippi* and did not understand how he could be so casual about having his life threatened. I certainly didn't feel too good about it.

I had to take the car I brought down and have it registered for Mississippi plates. This simple task of going in and having Mr. M., a black man on staff, register the car in his name, became a complicated procedure for the local county courthouse. The only way I could describe the courthouse is that it was much like a movie set of what an old, dusty, cheap second-grade movie would show a western courthouse to be. The clerk became suspicious when she saw Ed and called her supervisor, who started asking all sorts of irrelevant questions about why we got our cars in Boston and what we're going to use the car for. Ed returned to the questions *on the forms,* and didn't get involved in answering the questions which they had no right to ask in the first place. The county clerks insisted on having special papers made out and notarized and wanted to charge an extra surtax. We went to find the notary, who was an old man sleeping in his office. They insisted on calling Mr. M. "Jesse," because no self-respecting white man would address a black man by his last name and courtesy title. The only way they call him is by first name or "Hey, boy."

We then sat in on a meeting of welfare clients from the rurals—Utica, Hubbard, Clinton, Raymond and Edwards. I drove many of them home and saw what rural life was like. You can always tell where the blacks live because that is where the pavement ends and dirt roads begin. The poverty is unbelievable, worse that I had imagined—a little bit like *The Grapes of Wrath*: families crowded into hovels without water, sanitation, or electricity. The children show the results of malnutrition and stuffing themselves on the starches of surplus commodities. The distended bellies, bulging eyes, warped bone structure and running sores on hands and feet. Senator Eastland should see what this is like, and he would never again try to claim that there's no starvation in Mississippi.

We had a long talk that night about the differences of organization in the North and in the South. A young man who was a SNCC organizer during the 1963–64 confrontation was there and told us of the first restaurants and movie houses he had integrated and the torment he had to go through. Somehow you couldn't help but be proud of a guy like this; it was these young men, these college students, who won the rights for so many people at such a price. Never have so many owed so much to so few.

Ed pointed out something that is important for us to realize. There is practically no public transportation in the entire city of Jackson. The only bus lines they have are chartered very carefully to run from the black to the white community and back, so the buses can take the maids to their white masters each day for work. The clergy doesn't help very much because they simply lecture to the people. They tell them to pray, that "the meek shall inherit the earth," that "God helps those who help themselves," but God has not done too well for the black people in Mississippi for the last hundred years! The only hospital is "arbitrary"; the fees are set completely by whim. Babies are delivered by midwives for Negroes, by doctors for white people. There is no concept of preventive medicine. Malnutrition and such primitive diseases as pellagra and worms are abundant in black homes. Even when doctors give black people prescriptions, usually they cannot afford to fill them or buy the vitamins that are needed. Public opinion is entirely against the Negro. Both newspapers in Jackson are owned by the same family, which also owns, by coincidence, the local radio station. They take a conservative, anti-black, racist position so there is no free public opinion, no public forum to which blacks can turn for sympathy and support, or even for fair exposure. The NASW chapter is hardly a bastion of liberal thought or liberal action. Progressive young liberals go north. The children and the old people left behind aren't organized, are destitute, and without representation on any level of government, without transportation, phones, food, or medical care. It is hard sometimes to believe that this is the United States. I keep looking for the American Embassy—and I realize that there is none. The infant mortality rate for Negroes is tremendously high, partly because 40 per cent of black children are delivered by midwife (called the "granny lady"), while only 1/5 of 1 per cent of white children are delivered by midwife. This explains why Mississippi, in another one of its wonderful statistics, has the highest infant fatality rate in the nation. It shows the result of annually giving up 75 million dollars in federal welfare grants rather than accepting this money so badly needed for the children. "Washington," "Lyndon Johnson," and the "federal government" are all swear words in Mississippi. "We like states rights down here, we like *local* government and noninterference; in short, we like to preserve the good old Southern way of life."

## Tuesday

Today we got our first exposure to the Department of Welfare. We reported at eight o'clock in the morning to the welfare office to meet with fifteen clients who have joined the Hinds County Welfare Rights Movement. It is hard to describe welfare in Mississippi. In New York City, the average aid-to-dependent-children payment is $208.25 a month; in Mississippi it is $31.74. That means that an *entire* family lives and pays for rent, food, health, medical supplies and education on $31.74 a month (or approximately $1 a day per family). The welfare workers are all untrained; whites are automatically taken out of turn before blacks; clients are often cruelly abused; unauthorized questions are asked, and people are accepted or denied welfare arbitrarily. A client will be casually told, "Come back tomorrow, we're too busy today." An old man in his eighties will be told when applying for old age assistance, "Oh, I'm sorry, we're not giving any more old age assistance this month; why don't you come back after Christmas." Customarily he says, "Yes, ma'am" and goes home.

The supervisor was prepared for us because this was one of the two special welfare days each week on which the Hinds County Welfare Rights Movement was given special privileges. They had won the right to sit in with clients during interviews with the caseworkers after a long battle launched several weeks before. The workers still try to convince the clients that they don't need representation in the interview, but the clients say "Yes, I want this man to be with me." The basic form that the workers fill out is twelve pages long, and the ADC client has to fill out *27 pages of forms in all.* The system is archaic—and the people running it are even more out of date than the forms. I went in with a woman whose husband had deserted her years before, so she had to fill out Department of Welfare Form 236. It is difficult to believe, but this woman had to fill out that form not in triplicate, not even in quintuplicate, but in *24 copies* with 24 original signatures. When I asked the worker what happened to the 24 copies, he could not account for more than four. One woman came in to add a child to her welfare grant which she was already receiving. It took two hours, and she had to fill out forty-seven separate pieces of paper in order to receive an additional $2.27 a month. We made a lot of noise and caused a lot of trouble when they took a white client out of turn, and then filed for a fair hearing. This upset the local county agent very much, which is exactly, of course, what we were there to do. I can see that it's going to take some time for a Northerner like myself to get used to this community.

There is one power structure and it is monolithic; there are *never* any scandals, there is no dissent, there is no muckraking from the press, there are no unions; everything is owned by whites who protect each other. There are no challenging political parties and no challenge to a tradition of Protestant Christianity. It is a sick, monolithic society. It needs an injection of new blood. It seems to be dying from its own decay. The trouble is, it takes too many black lives to the grave.

That afternoon we went to a meeting organized by a group of Catholic priests to plan new services for the community. It is a difficult meeting to describe. The local head of the Community Health and Welfare Council spoke and made a complete fool of himself. He obviously didn't know a thing about services in the community, had never gotten together with poor people, and was ridiculed, *even* by the whites. There was a good middle-of-the-road rabbi (whose synagogue and home have since been bombed), the usual group of comfortable white ministers, a Negro minister (who looked more white than black), and a bunch of white "Crackers" sitting in the back waiting for someone to mention the word "integration." The priest who ran the meeting handled it very skillfully, and may succeed in developing some new programs and services. Just the fact that blacks and whites were sitting in the same room discussing a problem was some sort of accomplishment, and that they could use the word *rights* without having a rebellion from the white Crackers was perhaps an auspicious beginning. We went off for a pizza and a long bull session well into the night.

## Wednesday

With only four hours' sleep, we were tired. But we had to start early and be at the welfare office before eight. We flooded the workers with twenty-five clients. We insisted that any client they didn't take must be given an appointment for the next day, first thing in the morning. I went in and sat with a client while he was being interviewed for old age assistance. He was a very old man with gnarled hands, ninety-two years old, with no income at all. He lived out in the rurals in a shack with kerosene lamps, an outhouse, and had to walk a quarter of a mile to haul water in pails from a pump. He couldn't read or write, had never been to school in his life, and was a real product of the plantation way of life. His clothes were torn and his face was tired. He had few teeth. He told me later that a white man had knocked them out about twenty years before when he forgot to say "sir" when turning his bale of cotton in to market. The few teeth he had were pretty much decayed and I asked him if he had ever been to a dentist, and he said he had never been to one. He had Medicare, but when he goes to the white doctor, the doctor takes $5 from him, and then files for Medicare himself—so that the doctor not only collects from the patient but from the government as well. The patient (not being able to read or write) is none the wiser. But he kept questioning me as to why Medicare was any good if he *still* had to pay! We're going to have to look into this. Everyone cheats the black man. Here is a ninety-two-year-old man with no money, no health and no dignity. When he was turned down for welfare (which we're going to protest with a fair hearing), he broke down and cried. He had been abandoned by a society that had not given him an education, health, a decent home, electricity, running water, happiness or pride. He, at ninety-two, was just "Hey, boy." He was "The Other America."

I then went in with a woman applying for aid to dependent children. She tried to get into the work experience program but she had six children and they would only take women who have less than five children. (This means that all the hard-core families are ruled out by the work experience program.) The worker said she was too busy these days to visit Mrs. B., so she would have to wait for her welfare "for another couple of months." I insisted that the worker make a visit and determination within thirty days or we would file for a fair hearing. The worker became upset and began to stutter and shake: Were we accusing her of being dishonest? Were we accusing her of not caring? I answered that that was *exactly* what we were accusing her of, and that's what we would accuse her of at a fair hearing if she didn't get busy.

I then asked the worker what would the client live on

today and tomorrow until she got on welfare? What would she pay her rent with? The worker said very callously, "I don't know and I don't care; there is nothing we can do; we don't have general assistance in Mississippi; she'll do all right; she'll find something to eat." I then said to the worker (who was an immense woman), "Well, she doesn't seem to be eating as well as you; I don't think you know what hunger is all about." I told her, "I bet you have eaten today as much as my client ate all last week." The worker got mad, but before we left we reminded her that we were filing for a fair hearing because of her conduct, which was disgraceful and unprofessional. Mrs. B. got her case processed in record-breaking speed.

We went to a private social agency to get a "special food grant" which they often give. The worker there—untrained, old and incompetent—called my client by her first name. She asked to be called by her last name and courtesy title. In the middle of the interview the lunch bell rang, and the worker simply left my client sitting in the room and said she'd be back in an hour after lunch. I demanded that she go back and finish the interview and have her lunch later. I said, "A client's life is more important than lunch." She became furious. She told my client that she would never get help if she came with me or someone from our agency again. I said that we would make an appointment with her supervisor next week at which time we would make a judgment of her professional competence to continue in her present position. It had a tremendous impact on my client—not only that we were able to get money for food and for rent from the woman (who by now was trembling), but also that I (a white person) was willing to tell off another white person in her presence. Down South, whites never argue in the presence of blacks because it involves a loss of face.

That afternoon I went to meet Ed at the local county courthouse where a trial was going to be held for Neighborhood Youth Corps youngsters who had been arrested by the executive director of the local poverty program! The director of this local poverty agency was an insensitive, racist-oriented, right-wing man whom they were trying to get replaced. While the courtroom is no longer legally segregated, normally the whites sit on one side and the blacks on the other. They are handled differently, treated differently, and the law is dealt out differently. I had to laugh when I looked on the outside of the courthouse building and saw the phrase "Equal justice under the law for all." It seemed such a mockery. You can imagine our surprise when the judge dismissed the case against all sixteen neighborhood youth workers and dismissed it "northern style"; I mean that the white judge did not lecture the youngsters to be "good niggers," or threaten them with punishment or abuse. Usually when a white man lets a Negro get away with something he has to give him a lecture and talk down to him so that he knows never to be an "uppity nigger" again. To dismiss the case was a real surprise. And to dismiss it northern style was an even greater victory for the black youngsters (who had staged a sit-in in the office of the director of the poverty program).

That night we had another organizing and strategy session with Ed. He is an imaginative and creative community organizer, and listening to him is a tremendous learning experience. We went to bed at 3 A.M., very tired, with a knowledge that at six o'clock another day would begin.

## Thursday

We were sleepy but were off to Rankin County which adjoins Hinds. Ed had decided that the movement had to spread and that we would begin organizing clients and taking on the welfare department in Rankin County as well. The county seat in Rankin is the town of Brandon. It is a small, sleepy town where every new face is noticed and reported. At 8 A.M. we had fifteen people in the office to apply. The county agent was quite surprised, but polite and prepared to use last names and courtesy titles. Obviously they had called over to Hinds County to find out who we were and Hinds County had warned them to be careful because we cause trouble. One of the first things we noticed was that the rest rooms were segregated. Inside the office was a rest room that the employees used which was WHITE ONLY and outside were separate rest rooms with signs saying COLORED WOMEN and COLORED MEN. We filed a fair hearing right away on this. We got the clients talking while they were waiting and pointed out to their great joy that there was much more fear on the faces of the workers than on the faces of the clients. The agent had one of the sheriffs come in and pace up and down the office to intimidate the clients. They looked a little scared at first as he stared into each one of their faces with that knowing look of "Nigger, I won't forget your face if you cause trouble." I purposely spoke very loud in talking with the group telling them about intimidation, about the FBI, about how President Kennedy died for them, about the Civil Rights Act and other more obscure federal statutes (some of which I made up as I went along), which over-whelmed the sheriff, and he walked away. His attempts at intimidation had backfired. In my first interview in Rankin with a client, I immediately established that I was a *professional* social worker, which stuns and scares an entirely untrained staff. I took over the interview completely, saying of course, that with my background, I knew I could be help-ful. I made frequent mention of fair hearings. When the worker said, "Oh, we've never had many of those fair hear-ings out *here*," I made sure to mention that we had just filed 175 fair hearings in Hinds County last month. The worker reached for some pills in her drawer and went to the fountain. The client didn't miss the fact that the worker had to take tranquilizers. For a moment, the black woman was on top and the white woman was on bottom.

All in all, it was a good day in Rankin County for our first encounter. We achieved recognition of the clients' right to have a worker accompany them in the interview, and their right to be called by last name and courtesy title. We increased their intake to nineteen (which is more than twice their daily load) ; we filed many fair hearings, and we deseg-regated the washrooms. The last was a memorable and cathartic experience. When one of the black women had to go to the bathroom, we suggested that there was no need for her to use the Negro bathroom, that she could use the white one because in this country we all use the same bathrooms regardless of our race. She walked somewhat timidly toward the "white" bathroom, with the organizer walking behind her. Several white workers and secretaries came out to watch and see if a black woman would really try to go into their all-white bathroom. And she did. The workers became scared, rushed into the county agent's office, and I was prepared for some action. But they were so overwhelmed that any Negro would *try* to do such a thing that they didn't have an appropriate response. Pretty soon, all the women—whether they wanted to go to the bathroom or not, lined up outside the door so they could get a taste of fresh towels, good soap and clean toilets.

That night, I decided to see a movie. George, one of the young SNCC men, wanted to go see *Hurry Sundown*, so we went together. It is a film about white hostility in the Deep South, with the Negroes as victors! I was amazed that they were willing to show such a film in Mississippi. When we went into the theater downtown, we noticed that while there were no "colored" and "white" sections marked off, all the black people sat in one corner in the back where they were supposed to. George (who is black) walked right into the center of the movie house and sat down in one of the best seats. I followed. As soon as we sat down, every white in the entire row got up and left, moving to another seat. As soon as our aisle cleared, the one in front of us cleared and the one in back of us too. Then two aisles in front of us cleared and two aisles behind us cleared. Pretty soon we sat alone. George is pretty spirited and he would often yell out, "Hey man, we're winning," when the blacks won out over the whites in the film. The hostility was tremendous; you could cut it with a knife. I prepared for flying bottles, but none came. If it weren't 1967 and the best movie house in Jackson, I'm sure we would have walked out of that theater with cuts and bruises. But we were lucky. The content of the movie, of course, heightened the existing tension and we didn't waste much time getting out of the movie house when the picture was over.

## Friday

Friday was a quiet day. I did some proposal planning for a Manpower Training and Job Development Program, and with a related health and social service project Ed was interested in. I wrote a couple of letters, did some laundry, made out a couple of reports, did some phone calls and prepared for a staff meeting that evening. Ed and his wife are going off to Gulfport for a well-earned weekend tonight, and we volunteers will stand by on duty for the weekend.

## Saturday

On Saturday, we went out to Rankin County to meet with many of the families who would come to the welfare day at the Rankin County office. Because of the success of our initial day, they brought many friends and it was a large meeting in the back of an old wooden church in the poorest black section of the rurals. The meeting was an exciting one. There were a great number of *men* there, which is something we've had difficulty in achieving even in New York. We role-played an interview at a welfare office. A fellow volunteer took the role of a worker assisting a client. A client who had done very well yesterday played her own role as client, and I took the role of a typical welfare investigator. Role play works well. The reaction of the people was very vivid. When I called Mrs. L. by her first name and accused her of lying, she began to react! It's going to be hard to get black people to talk back to whites, but by doing so in a relatively safe role-play situation, they prepare for the much harder fight at the county welfare office. Then the leader of the group decided that he wanted an all-black committee to meet with the county agent and present a set of demands based on their experiences. He said these demands would be called a Bill of Rights because they would list rights as welfare clients that they had always been denied. Their Bill of Rights read as follows:

1. Clients will not be cut off welfare without written notification and explanation of reasons for this action.

2. Clients will not be removed from commodities (surplus food) without written notification and explanation.

3. Clients will not be cut off welfare simply because they sell a cow or a single load of timber.

4. Clients have the right to be accompanied by a representative of their choice in meeting with the Department of Welfare.

5. Every application must be taken when a client comes in to apply. (In other words, you can't be told, "We're not taking old age applications this month.")

6. Welfare will not tell the clients to do things like build a house or make repairs and then when they do this, cut them off welfare for having done so. (This is a favorite game.)

7. All clients must be called by their last names and courtesy titles.

8. All washrooms must be integrated.

9. The next welfare worker to be hired must be a qualified Negro.

10. We want the law to be carried out equally for everyone and without threats or intimidation.

11. All clients must be taken in the order which they come in regardless of race.

12. The Rankin County Welfare Rights Movement will be given one regular day a week, and the first twelve clients to be seen will be members of the Welfare Rights Movement.

13. A regular monthly meeting should be established by the county agent with representatives of the Welfare Rights Movement to discuss mutual problems and work toward solutions.

One can see that this was an historic document. In one sense it was sad that anyone needed a bill of rights like this in 1967. On the other hand, it was a sign of tremendous courage that local black people, oppressed for two hundred years, would come up with these ideas in the rurals of central Mississippi.

When we left for New York, we were older and wiser. Whatever our contribution, it surely had been very small. But we had learned a lot about people, about community organization, and the common plight of men who are not free.

## Study Questions

1. What do you think of the worker's initial reactions to life in the rurals, at the courthouse, etc.? Was he very naïve? What are the emotional adjustments that a worker must make when he first experiences what he has only read before in books?

2. What are the implications for community organizing of the "sociology" of the setting? Is it likely that the worker will have to approach his tasks differently in a southern, rural setting? Why? Are there universally applicable principles of community organization?

3. Is the system of public welfare administration described here more archaic than you have experienced in other settings? Explain.

4. Discuss the situation of the ninety-two-year-old client applying for assistance in terms of how you as a worker in a neighborhood service center would go about helping him. How would you go about developing a social study, psychosocial diagnosis and treatment plan? What resources might be available to you to help him?

5. Do you think a work experience program is justified in ruling out women with more than four children? What are the arguments on both sides of the case? Where would you stand on this issue?

6. Was the worker with Mrs. B. justified in accusing the

welfare agent of not caring about the client? Was he being sensitive to the dilemma of the agent and the needs of a public agency?

7. What do you think about the worker's handling of the case of Mrs. B. at the private social agency? Was there a purpose in his deliberate staging of an emotional confrontation? Would you have handled it differently?

8. Since there is a Public Accommodations Section to the federal Civil Rights Act, how could a courthouse have segregated rest rooms? Do you think this was the exception in courthouses throughout the state, or the rule?

9. What was the worker trying to accomplish in the interview session he describes in Rankin County? Do you think he was successful? Why was such an effort made to integrate the washrooms? What (if any) was the significance of the clients' using the washroom that had been reserved for the all-white staff?

10. What was George trying to show or accomplish by his actions at the movie? What would your reaction have been if you had been the white worker?

11. Why do you think there were so many *men* at the welfare rights meeting out in Rankin, when there tend to be so few involved in welfare rights activity up North?

12. What are the advantages and limitations of role play as a training device in community organization? When would you choose to use it; when would you not—and why?

13. The worker describes a single week here in his experience as a social work volunteer. Do you feel such an experience will be valuable (or not) for a worker who will return to working in an urban setting up North? What aspects of the experience might be functional? Dysfunctional? Why?

# About the Contributors

Paul A. Kurzman is a social worker with a fondness for both organizing and administration. He has served as Senior Community Organizer with the Two Bridges Neighborhood Council on New York's Lower East Side and as the Acting Executive Director of the Lower East Side Neighborhoods Association (LENA). He received an A.B. from Princeton, his master's degree from the Columbia University School of Social Work, and a Ph.D. in public administration from New York University. Dr. Kurzman has served as a social welfare consultant in both the public and private sector, and has written extensively for the professional journals of social work, community development and public administration. Presently he is Assistant Commissioner of the Youth Services Agency in New York City's Human Resources Administration, and Director of the City's $30-million-a-year Neighborhood Youth Corps program.

George A. Wiley began his career as a chemistry professor at Syracuse University and the University of California, later switching to social welfare and community organization. After serving as Associate National Director of the Congress on Racial Equality (CORE), Dr. Wiley became Executive

Director of the National Welfare Rights Organization (NWRO). The NWRO, a national organization of public assistance recipients, is based in Washington, D.C., with a network of over 300 chapters spread throughout the country.

Ronald M. Arundell received his MSW from the Fordham University School of Social Service and served for three years as a social work officer in the United States Public Health Service. He is now living on a commune and serving as a free-lance community organizer on health and welfare issues in Cincinnati, Ohio.

Judith White Beyman served as Director of St. Mary's Community Services in New York City after graduating from the Columbia University School of Social Work with a major in community organization. Mrs. Beyman has long been active in welfare rights and now is a counselor with Malcolm-King Harlem College Extension in New York City.

Barbara A. Schram is an alumna of Antioch College and the Columbia University School of Social Work. After extensive experience in group work and community organization, Miss Schram became Administrator of the Two Bridges Parent Development Program in New York City, and subsequently, supervisor of graduate social work students in New York City's Human Resources Administration. Miss Schram presently is a social work consultant and doctoral student in the School of Education at Harvard University.

Ted Seaver served for three years as Director of the Community Development Agency, the action arm of the Schwerner Fund in Jackson, Mississippi. A graduate of the University of Wisconsin, Mr. Seaver now is Assistant Director of the Neighborhood Opportunity Centers, Inner City Development Project, Milwaukee, Wisconsin. In addition, he is active as an organizer of the militant Milwaukee Tenants'

Union, and in building low-income black-white coalitions to press for social change.

Heather Smith received her MSW from the University of Wisconsin at Madison and then went South to work on the staff of the Community Development Agency in Jackson, Mississippi. Specializing in welfare rights, she gave staff service to the Hinds County Welfare Rights Movement. She is presently a welfare rights organizer in Berkeley, California.

Jeffrey R. Solomon received his master's degree in social work from Columbia University and has been active in the area of rehabilitation. At present he is Assistant Executive Director of Altro Health and Rehabilitation Services in New York City, and President of Social Consult, Inc., a social welfare consultant firm that specializes in program development and evaluation.

Gardenia White was Parent Education Coordinator of the Two Bridges Parent Development Program on New York's Lower East Side. A mother of three teen-agers, she has been active in educational issues in New York City and has served as a paraprofessional consultant to private social agencies and the Queens College Institute for Community Studies. Mrs. White most recently served as a case aide at the Mental Hygiene Clinic of the Henry Street Settlement, and is now a consultant with Teachers, Incorporated.